DEFENDING A
HIGHER LAW

DEFENDING A
HIGHER LAW

---

*Why We Must Resist
Same-Sex "Marriage"
and the Homosexual Movement*

by

TFP Committee on American Issues

THE AMERICAN SOCIETY FOR THE DEFENSE
OF TRADITION, FAMILY AND PROPERTY — TFP
SPRING GROVE, PENN. 17362

Cover illustration: Moses with the Ten Commandments by Gustave Doré

Copyright © 2004 The American Society for the Defense of Tradition, Family and Property®—TFP®
1358 Jefferson Road, Spring Grove, Penn. 17362—(866) 661-0272
www.tfp.org

The American Society for the Defense of Tradition, Family and Property® and TFP® are registered names of The Foundation for a Christian Civilization, Inc., a 501(c)(3) tax-exempt organization.

ISBN: 1-877905-33-X
Library of Congress Control Number: 2004100055

Printed in Canada

This book is dedicated to the Holy Family, the sublime model for all families, and our sure guide in the reaction to the sexual revolution and homosexual offensive.

May the Blessed Mother intercede with Her Divine Son for all Americans committed to defend the sacred institutions of marriage and the family.

D I O C E S E
of NEW ULM

February 3, 2004

Mr. Thomas J. McKenna, Vice President
The American Society for the Defense of Tradition, Family and Property
1358 Jefferson Road
Spring Grove, PA 17362

Dear Mr. McKenna,

I am pleased to recommend the recent publication by The American Society for the Defense of Tradition, Family and Property (TFP) entitled *Defending a Higher Law: Why We Must Resist Same-Sex "Marriage" and the Homosexual Movement*. This work provides the historical background of the current political movement to legalize "homosexual unions" as well as a systematic presentation of the arguments put forth by the proponents of such unions. It carefully analyzes their proposals and demonstrates how those notions are lacking in a true understanding of the nature of the human person as well as the meaning of marital intercourse which is the foundation for determining what constitutes the covenant of marriage.

The study also addresses the important influence of the media in portraying "homosexual unions" as a kind of "civil right," the denial of which demonstrates a lack of compassion on the part of society or, worse, a form of unjust discrimination. In point of fact, a correct understanding of the social order ought to bring about a defense of the integrity and well-being of the family as the basic building block for society's infrastructure. To equivocate on the meaning of marriage as anything less than the permanent commitment of a "two-in-one flesh" covenant between a man and a woman is to attack the stability of family life and to threaten the very underpinnings of society.

While all citizens can by the use of reason arrive at the above conclusions, Christian believers have an even clearer perspective on the matter from the teachings of Sacred Scripture, the witness of the saints and the constant teaching of the Church. All three of these areas are likewise systematically presented by TFP's new publication.

My hope is that *Defending a Higher Law* will be widely read and have a positive effect on prohibiting legislative initiatives aimed at legally redefining the meaning of marriage.

With every good wish, I am

Cordially yours in Christ,

+ John C. Nienstedt

The Most Reverend John C. Nienstedt
Bishop of New Ulm

What people are saying about
Defending a Higher Law:

In the difficult cultural situation in the United States and indeed in the whole Western world, anyone who is interested in the deterioration of Christian morality, especially in the field of sexual morality and God's will in matrimony, cannot ignore the contribution of the book *Defending a Higher Law: Why We Must Resist Same-Sex "Marriage" and the Homosexual Movement* and what it brings to bear on these issues which are so vital for the future of humanity.

The Most Reverend Fabian W. Bruskewitz
Bishop of Lincoln, Neb.

With an enormous amount of confusion and misinformation surrounding homosexual inclinations and relationships, the issue of homosexuality is very highly emotionally charged. Seemingly any discussion which challenges homosexual behaviors is quickly assigned to the "homophobic" file. *Defending a Higher Law: Why We Must Resist Same Sex "Marriage" and the Homosexual Movement* does an excellent job of clarifying the seriously misunderstood religious and social aspects of a homosexual lifestyle. I believe this book will help dispel the false perceptions which, unfortunately, have beclouded the minds of many, even solidly orthodox, Catholic men and women.

The Most Reverend Robert F. Vasa, Bishop of Baker, Ore.
Episcopal Advisor of the Catholic Medical Association

Defending a Higher Law is an informative , intelligent, enlightening guide to the issues raised by the gay movement. This is a book for all Americans who want to understand the many dimensions of this question.

Sandy Rios
President, Concerned Women for America

In its monograph *Defending a Higher Law: Why We Must Resist Same-Sex "Marriage" and the Homosexual Movement*, the TFP has raised issues which have long been suppressed in the dialogue over this question. It is an excellent primer for anyone wishing to understand the church's historical position on homosexuality. It is the definitive answer to those who would excuse the sin in the name of compassion.

Paul M. Weyrich
President, Free Congress Research
and Educational Foundation

Defending a Higher Law: Why We Must Resist Same Sex "Marriage" and the Homosexual Movement is a major educational resource for the socially concerned Catholic Reader. TFP's book clearly and accurately spells out the key issues and arguments exposing the pro-gay movement from both the Catholic and scientific perspective. TFP is to be applauded for its courageous stand.

Joseph Nicolosi, PhD
President, National Association for Research &
Therapy of Homosexuality (NARTH)

EUREKA! Finally a thoroughly objective, rational, logical and factual analysis of the homosexual myth currently permeating the modern society. This book exposes the fallacies of the "politically correct" crowd both within and without the Church. Using perennially valid philosophy and divinely revealed truths, this book validates the long held suspicion that a BIG LIE has been sold to the sociologists, psychologists and dissident moral theologians who seek to legitimize and normalize aberrant, unnatural and immoral behavior.

Rev. Fr. John Trigilio, Jr., PhD, ThD
President, Confraternity of Catholic Clergy
Host of EWTN's series Web of Faith and Council of Faith

The United States Federal Courts have, as this masterful book makes clear, displayed a gross dereliction of their duty to follow the Constitution. They have betrayed everything America once stood for by abandoning the natural law upon which its founding documents were grounded. This betrayal represents "…a major blow to America's Christian roots, the institution of the family, and the very foundation of morality and society." By revealing precisely what is wrong with America today *Defending a Higher Law: Why We Must Resist Same-Sex "Marriage" and the Homosexual Movement* strikes at the heel of the homosexual ideology. And by showing how homosexuality is being spread in America by a well organized movement of homosexuals with its anti-Christian ideology and studied methodology, this book gives us a powerful and useful weapon to oppose their offensive and to defend Christian values. We thank the American TFP for this extremely valuable weapon to use in the fight to defend the family, the Church, and our nation.

Joseph M. Scheidler
Founder and National Director, Pro-Life Action League
Recipient of Legatus' 2003 Pro-Life Award

Defending a Higher Law is essential for understanding the gay rights movement and the current push for homosexual marriage. With an economy of words, this book lays out the roots of the gay rights movement, refutes the arguments for normalizing the lifestyle, defends marriage as the unique institution it is and underpins the whole process with the writings of the Saints, scriptural condemnations of homosexual sins and recent Vatican documents. This book will become a reference book for those who recognize the decline in our culture and are willing to fight for the restoration.

Mary Anne Hackett
President, Catholic Citizens of Illinois

ঝ CONTENTS ৪

Preliminary Remarks   XV

Introduction   1

ঝ PART I ৪
The Homosexual Revolution

Chapter 1
The Homosexual Movement:
Imposing a Moral Revolution   7

Chapter 2
Making the Link No One Wants to Make   11

Chapter 3
Origins of the Homosexual Movement:
The Strange Case of Harry Hay   15

Chapter 4
The Homosexual Network: Spinning a Web   21

Chapter 5
Exposing the Movement's Tactics: You Are the Target   31

Chapter 6
Why Same-Sex "Marriage" Matters: Validating the
Homosexual Ideology   43

Chapter 7
Making the Immoral Moral   49

Chapter 8
Mystical Eroticism: The Hidden Side of the Rainbow   53

ঝ PART II ৪
Answering the Homosexual
Movement's Arguments

Chapter 9
The True Purpose of the Sexual Act   67

Chapter 10
The Impossibility of True Homosexual Love   77

Chapter 11
Answering the Movement's Scientific Arguments   83

Chapter 12
Answering Twelve Arguments Used to Push the
Homosexual Agenda   95

Chapter 13
The Romantic Myth and the Tragic Reality   105

Chapter 14
A False Concept of Compassion   117

Chapter 15
Refuting Revisionist Biblical Scholars—Sodom
Was Punished for Its Homosexuality   123

‌‌ ✒ PART III ✒
Natural Law and Church Teaching
Have Always Condemned Homosexuality

Chapter 16
Natural Law: Man's Necessary Point of Reference   139

Chapter 17
The Voice of the Apostles   147

Chapter 18
Church Fathers and Doctors Condemn Homosexuality   153

Chapter 19
Ecclesiastical Discipline:
Translating Words into Action   165

Chapter 20
Recent Church Condemnations of Homosexuality   173

Chapter 21
The Vatican's 2003 Condemnation   177

Conclusion   187

Appendix
Are We Still "One Nation Under God"?   191

Index   203

৩ BOXES ৪

- Georgetown: Two Examples of Liberal Tolerance — 28
- "Homophobia"–A Semantic Weapon in the Cultural War — 35
- The Ten Percent Myth — 40
- Vices Turned into Gods — 59
- A New Gnostic World — 62
- Our Lord Elevated Matrimony to the Supernatural Level — 70
- The Primary End of Marriage — 73
- "If God Didn't Exist, Everything Would Be Possible"–Dostoevsky — 145
- The Ugandan Martyrs: Saints Charles Lwanga and Companions — 185

PRELIMINARY REMARKS

In writing this book, we have no intention to defame or disparage anyone. We are not moved by personal hatred against any individual. In intellectually opposing individuals or organizations promoting the homosexual agenda, our only intent is the defense of marriage, the family and the precious remnants of Christian civilization in society.

As practicing Catholics, we are filled with compassion and pray for those who struggle against unrelenting and violent temptation to sin, be it toward homosexual sin or otherwise. In describing the physical, moral and spiritual consequences ensuing from sins of the flesh, we hope to counsel them away from sin, and provide them with insight to the necessity and beauty of the virtue of chastity that some may have never known.

We pray for those who fall into homosexual sin out of human weakness, that God may assist them with His grace. May they rise again, healed by a gaze from Our Divine Savior, to fall no more. In denouncing the ideology that pervades the homosexual movement, we hope to help them see how the movement may be exploiting them in its pursuit of ideological objectives with which they may not agree.

We are conscious of the enormous difference between these individuals who struggle with their weaknesses and strive to overcome them and others who transform their sin into a reason for pride, and try to impose their lifestyle on society as a whole, in flagrant opposition to traditional Christian morality and natural law.

However, we pray even for these. Yes, we pray for the radical activists pushing the homosexual agenda, even as we do everything permitted by law to block their efforts. We pray that, through the intercession of Mary Most Holy, the grace God gave Saint Paul on the road to Damascus be given them as well, so that they may come to see the errors they promote, sincerely reject them, convert to God and join us.

If, in the heat of the debate, what some might consider a sharp expression or caustic remark slipped by, it is not intentional. In this debate of national magnitude, dealing with a most grave and complex issue rife with delicate philosophical and theological nuances, one is not always successful in formulating ideas with the required needlepoint precision. This difficult task is further complicated by the time constraints imposed by galloping events.

In short, according to the famous expression attributed to Saint Augustine, we "hate the sin but love the sinner."[1] And to love the sinner, as the same Doctor of the Church explains, is to wish for him the best we can possibly desire for ourselves, namely, "that he may love God with a perfect affection."[2]

*   *   *

We will also not use the word *gay* as a synonym of *homosexual*, except when quoted, because the universal acceptance of this usage is a victory for the homosexual movement. In its battle for public acceptance, the movement shunned the word *homosexual* because of its association with morally reprehensible behavior. While efforts to replace it with the word *homophile* were not successful, the acceptance of the word *gay* was a valuable homosexual victory in the Cultural War. Prof. Livio Melina of the Pontifical Lateran University in Rome claims the word gay "is highly politicized and does not simply mean a homosexually oriented person but one who publicly adopts a homosexual 'lifestyle' and is committed to having it accepted by society as fully legitimate."[3]

*   *   *

---

1. Cf. Commentary on Psalm 119, www.ccel.org/schaff/npnf108.ii.CXIX.xv.html.
2. St. Augustine, *Of the Morals of the Catholic Church*, no. 49, www.newad vent.org/fathers/1401.htm.
3. Prof. Livio Melina, "Christian Anthropology and Homosexuality: Moral criteria for evaluating homosexuality," *L'Osservatore Romano*, weekly English edition, Mar. 12, 1997, p. 5.

The indiscriminate use of the word *homosexual* and its synonyms has generated much confusion in the public. Many times, it is unclear if it refers to someone with same-sex attraction only or if it refers to someone who practices homosexual acts.

This confusion favors the homosexual agenda. We cannot equate people with same-sex attraction who resist it and are chaste with those who engage in homosexual behavior. These are two distinct and essentially different moral realities.

Thus, we will use *homosexual* to refer only to those who practice homosexual acts and thereby deserve moral reprobation.

* * *

References to or quotes from persons, organizations, institutions or publications do not necessarily mean that we agree with their philosophical or religious positions. We adhere firmly to the Catholic Faith and morals and to the *philosophia perennis*, especially in its Thomistic expression.

* * *

For documentation purposes, we reference some web sites and publications with objectionable content and, therefore, feel obliged to warn the reader.

INTRODUCTION

The Supreme Court's June 26, 2003 decision in *Lawrence v. Texas* effectively denied the existence of God's Eternal Law and natural law, and established its own atheistic and anarchic "morality."[1]

The 6-3 majority recognized liberty as the supreme norm of human thought and action. "At the heart of liberty is the right to define one's own concept of existence, of meaning, of the universe, and of the mystery of human life."[2] In the name of this absolute freedom, the Court established a constitutionally protected right to the private practice of sodomy. Moreover, the bench erected the legal constructs for a future decision granting constitutional protection to same-sex "marriage" when it made the following assertions:

> Liberty presumes an autonomy of self that includes...certain intimate conduct....[3]
>
> Adults may choose to enter upon this relationship in the confines of their homes and their own private lives and still retain their dignity as free persons. When sexuality finds overt expression in intimate conduct with another person, the conduct can be but one element in a personal bond that is more enduring. The liberty protected by the Constitution allows

---

1. Emmanuel Kant formulated this anarchic "morality" in all its radicalism: "A person is properly subject to no other laws than those he lays down himself, either alone or in conjunction with others." Emmanuel Kant, *Introduction to the Metaphysic of Morals*, ethics.acusd.edu/Books/Kant/MetaMorals/NS/Kant_MM_NS.htm.

2. *Lawrence*, Opinion of the Court, p. 13. Here the Court quotes its decision in *Planned Parenthood of Southeastern Pa. v. Casey*. In this book, quotes from the Supreme Court's decision in *Lawrence v. Texas* are from the slip opinion available at http://a257.g.akamaitech.net/7/257/2422/26jun20031200/www.supremecourtus.gov/opinions/02pdf/02-102.pdf and are cited as "*Lawrence*," the specific judicial opinion, and the opinion page number.

3. *Lawrence*, Opinion of the Court, p. 1.

homosexual persons the right to make this choice....[4]

Persons in a homosexual relationship may seek autonomy for these purposes, just as heterosexual persons do.[5]

Given the premise of absolute liberty and "autonomy of self," the ruling's limitation of the new right to the practice of sodomy to people within "the confines of their homes" cannot be logically or long maintained. As Justice Antonin Scalia rightly noted in his dissenting opinion, this Supreme Court ruling effectively decreed "the end of all morals legislation."[6]

A CLASH OF TWO AMERICAS

Justice Scalia further observed in his dissent that the Supreme Court had taken "sides in the culture war."[7]

This Cultural War divides America.

On one side, there is a large sector of the American public which has long grieved over the abandonment of God's moral laws. These are Americans who subscribe to the general unwritten rule held since our founding that God must be revered, not offended, and that the source of our greatness is this reverence, and obedience to a Christian moral code based on the Ten Commandments and natural law.

For this Ten Commandments America, it is only too obvious that if America turns its back on God and His law, God will turn His back on America.

On the other side, there is a liberal America that subscribes to the philosophical principle of absolute liberty. This leads to the establishment of an atheistic and anarchic "morality," which shows increasing intolerance for what still remains of

---

4.   Ibid., p. 6.
5.   Ibid., p. 13.
6.   *Lawrence*, Scalia, J. dissenting, p. 15.
7.   Ibid., p. 18.

Christian civilization and the natural order in our culture and society. Among these precious remnants are the sacred institutions of marriage and the family.

SAME-SEX "MARRIAGE," A DECISIVE STEP IN THE HOMOSEXUAL OFFENSIVE

Citing *Lawrence* as precedent, the Massachusetts Supreme Judicial Court ruled November 18, 2003, in *Goodridge v. Department of Public Health*, that two men or two women have a right to marriage under the constitution of the Bay State.

Like *Lawrence*, the Massachusetts *Goodridge* decision reverberated throughout the land. It multiplied the problems created five months earlier by the Supreme Court's decision and riveted the attention of all on the homosexuality debate.

Both decisions were of vital importance to the homosexual movement. Indeed, the movement must persuade public opinion that homosexuality is normal, albeit different. However, homosexuality will never be fully accepted as normal as long as homosexual partners cannot "marry." Thus, the movement gradually strives to reach this psychological milestone. Since it cannot achieve same-sex "marriage" immediately, the movement works for civil unions, domestic partnerships or partnership benefits, all of which are packaged as concessions, but actually are stepping stones across the river of public opposition.

STRATEGIES FOR VICTORY

The successful defense of traditional marriage and the family by Ten Commandments America will halt the homosexual offensive. However, to be victorious, the broad coalition now defending marriage and the family in this Cultural War must work hard to dispel the confusion shrewdly spread around the issue by the homosexual movement. We must refute the sophisms, myths and doctrinal errors that psychologically hinder many Americans from joining us in the fray.

The American Society for the Defense of Tradition, Family and Property (TFP) is publishing this book as a contribution to the coalition's overall effort. In this work, we will delve into the homosexual movement's agenda and its short- and long-term objectives. We will discuss its tactics, answer its arguments and untwist the misleading spin romanticizing the homosexual lifestyle. We will show how the movement has a worldview based on a false morality and a neopagan mystical eroticism that is completely opposed to Christianity and natural law.

SOCIETY'S MORAL
FOUNDATIONS MUST BE RESTORED

The most profound reason for the homosexual movement's impressive victories, however, lies not in its strength, but in our weakness. This weakness is the result of a gradual decades-long effort to blur the distinction between good and evil, or right and wrong. This effort has led to a generalized loss of the sense of sin, and, consequently, declining standards of public morality.

An effective reaction to the homosexual offensive must strive, therefore, to reverse this underlying moral problem. It must reinvigorate society's moral foundations, which must be firmly based on the Ten Commandments and unchanging natural law. It must create the moral climate whereby homosexuality will be rejected.

To the measure that Christian morality is restored in individuals and society as a whole, the homosexual offensive will weaken and eventually suffocate, like a raging fire deprived of oxygen.

Then will God reign in the hearts of men, and the country can expect from His bounty every grace and blessing. Then, whatever courts may rule, America will in fact be "one nation under God."

PART I
The Homosexual Revolution

CHAPTER 1
The Homosexual Movement:
Imposing a Moral Revolution

Throughout history, groups of homosexuals have at times acquired political and especially cultural influence.

Perhaps the most striking example is the group of homosexual or bisexual artists and writers who left their mark on the Renaissance. They reintroduced the so-called Greek vice[1] in literature and the fine arts. This was particularly noticeable in the latter where the obsession with masculine nudity led artists to flaunt it in the most revealing poses. Both masculine and feminine figures manifested a clearly androgynous note. In spite of their bulging muscles, painting and sculptures of men showed them with a soft and effeminate character, while those of women displayed unbecoming masculinity.[2]

FOR THE FIRST TIME SOCIETY
FACES A HOMOSEXUAL MOVEMENT

For the first time, however, in the history of the Christian West, and perhaps humanity, society faces not just scattered groups of influential homosexuals, but an organized, visible movement of avowed homosexuals who not only boast of their habits but unite in an attempt to impose their ideology on society.

This is the *homosexual movement*—a vast network of organizations, pressure groups, radical intellectuals and

---

1. This is the name given to homosexuality because of its pervasiveness in ancient Greece.
2. Aretino, a humanist writer, wrote Michelangelo in 1542 praising his painting of Venus because "it depicted a goddess whose female body had 'the male's musculature, such that she is moved by virile and womanly feelings.'" European -: Renaissance, www.glbtq.com/arts/eur_art7_renaissance,3.html; Cf. James M. Saslow, *Ganymede in the Renaissance: Homosexuality in Art and Society* (New Haven, Conn.: Yale University Press, 1986); *Luciano Bottoni, Leonardo e l'Androgino* (Milan: Franco Angeli, 2002).

activists who strive to impose changes in laws, customs, morals and mentalities, so that homosexuality is not only tolerated but also accepted as good and normal. Hence, movement activists pressure society to legalize both the practice and the public manifestations of homosexuality, such as same-sex "marriage," while relentlessly assailing those who defend traditional morals.[3]

NOT A CIVIL RIGHTS MOVEMENT, BUT A MORAL REVOLUTION

Many believe the cultural battle over homosexuality is strictly a matter of civil rights. The homosexual movement does not despise the tactical advantages this perception secures. However, it seeks much more: a complete inversion of public morality. Writing in the *Chicago Free Press*, homosexual activist Paul Varnell affirms:

> The fundamental controverted issue about homosexuality is not discrimination, hate crimes or domestic partnerships, but the morality of homosexuality.
>
> Even if gays obtain non-discrimination laws, hate crimes law and domestic partnership benefits, those can do little to counter the underlying moral condemnation which will continue to fester beneath the law and generate hostility, fuel hate crimes, support conversion therapies, encourage gay youth suicide and inhibit the full social acceptance that is our goal.

---

3. For example, the web site of the *National Gay and Lesbian Task Force* offers a booklet titled *Know Thy Enemy: Quotes About the Sodomy Ruling and the Same-Sex Marriage Backlash*, July 28, 2003, by Michelle Klemens and Sheri A. Lunn. The site summarizes the book, saying: "The first in a series of compendiums exposing the vitriolic reactions of those who would deny lesbian, gay, bisexual and transgender people equal rights under the law. This report compiles quotes by everyone from Jerry Falwell to Rick Santorum and will be updated online on a regular basis." www.ngltf.org/library/index.cfm.

On the other hand, if we convince people that homosexuality is fully moral, then all their inclination to discriminate, engage in gay-bashing or oppose gay marriage disappears. Gay youths and adults could readily accept themselves.

So the gay movement, whether we acknowledge it or not, is not a civil rights movement, not even a sexual liberation movement, but a moral revolution aimed at changing people's view of homosexuality.[4]

4. Paul Varnell, "Defending Our Morality," *Chicago Free Press*, Aug. 16, 2000, http://indegayforum.org/authors/varnell/varnell37.html. (Our emphasis.)

CHAPTER 2
Making the Link No One Wants to Make

To understand the current homosexual revolution properly, we must see it within the broader picture of the sexual revolution.

Chastity, modesty and temperance—distinctive signs of Christian civilization—have given way to an unbridled quest for carnal pleasure and an unimaginable display of the human body.

This obsession for the sexual permeates our culture. Be it literature, fashion, entertainment, advertising or simply common speech and behavior, almost everything today is branded with this erotic stamp. Today's hypersexualized world has become a perfect hotbed for every form of sexual aberration.

DETACHING SENTIMENT FROM REASON

The sexual revolution of the sixties was prepared by a century of cultural developments where sentiment was detached from reason. In this regard, the Romantic School of literature and the arts celebrated a general exaltation of emotion over reason and the senses over the intellect.

In so doing, romance and love became the highest ideal. In the name of love and passion, every rule and social convention could be broken. When applied to morality, this mentality was devastating, since adultery and even prostitution could be rationalized and even acclaimed.[1]

---

1. George P. Landow, Professor of English and Art History at Brown University, writes about the philosophical and religious implications of Romanticism: "For the first time, philosophers no longer urged that the healthy human mind is organized hierarchically with reason, like a king, ruling will and passions. Reason now shares rule with feelings or emotions… For art and literature: the emotions become the proper subject of the arts…For religion: …Christianity's doctrine of Original Sin and human depravity must be wrong. Christianity and religion in general appear founded on an error." *Emotionalist Moral Philosophy: Sympathy and the Moral Theory that Overthrew Kings*, www.victorianweb.org/philosophy/phil4.html.

Such themes mark modern literature. Thousands of romantic novels and films present highly emotive and sentimental plots. A typical example of this is Alexandre Dumas's novel *The Lady of the Camellias* (1848), which revolves around a glamorous upper class prostitute. Despite its blatantly immoral characters, the novel enjoyed huge success worldwide. Verdi turned it into an opera, *La Traviata* (1853), which enjoyed equal success. Later, the novel inspired several Hollywood movies, the most famous being *Camille* (1936) starring Greta Garbo.

THE SEXUAL REVOLUTION: FROM SENTIMENT TO CARNAL SENSATION

This prolonged overemphasis on sentiment and the erosion of morals prepared the way for the next step: the unbridled, hedonistic pleasure of the senses. This was pleasure sought for its own sake—even when unaccompanied by sentiment or emotion—simply because it felt good.

In 1953, Hugh Hefner founded *Playboy*. Unabashedly hedonistic, this magazine "was a seminal influence on the 'sexual revolution' of the 1960s."[2]

Another contributing factor was the discovery and mass marketing of the contraceptive pill:

In May 1960, the FDA approved the sale of a pill that arguably would have a greater impact on American culture than any other drug in the nation's history. For women across the country, the contraceptive pill was liberating: it allowed them to pursue careers, fueled the feminist and pro-choice movements and encouraged more open attitudes towards sex.[3]

---

2. S.v. "Hefner, Hugh," in *Britannica Concise Encyclopedia*, www.britannica.com/ebc/article?eu=392129.
3. www.pbs.org/wgbh/amex/pill/filmmore/index.html.

THE HIPPIE MOVEMENT AND STUDENT REVOLT SERVE AS STANDARD-BEARERS

The separation of sexual activity from procreation, facilitated by the contraceptive pill, sparked a sexual explosion. The hippie movement and the student revolt that swept across America and the world during the sixties became the symbols of this urge for total sexual freedom. A revolutionary slogan painted on the walls of Paris's Sorbonne University aptly summarized this anarchic spirit: *Défense d'interdire* (It is forbidden to forbid). While the two differed from many standpoints, the hippie and student movements of the sixties were united in their rejection of the "establishment."[4] A 1999 *Time* magazine article reads:

> What was needed, they sang, was a revolution. Love and marriage—which once went together like a horse and carriage—were no longer a cool combination. The flared and freely 60s generation seized liberation of the flesh as its hot gospel; free love in freefall. In 1968 Paris—one year after France legalized the pill—the cry was *Jouissez sans entraves*, the carnal equivalent of today's *Just Do It*.[5]

At the heart of the sexual revolution is a revolt against all norms of morality that temper or restrain man's disordered passions. Indeed, in a society where "it is forbidden to forbid," morality has no place and unbridled instincts become the norm

---

4. This revolutionary thought was fed by authors such as Herbert Marcuse especially in *Eros and Civilization* (1955), Wilhem Reich in *Dialectical Materialism and Psychoanalysis* (1929), which mixed the theories of Marx and Freud and Charles Reich in *The Greening of America* (1970).

5. Rod Usher, "Revels Without a Cause," *Time*, Aug. 16, 1999. *Jouissez sans entraves* (Pleasure without restraint in English) was another slogan of the May 1968 revolt that was painted on the walls of the University of Paris. Cf. www.les-ours.com/novel/mai68.

of conduct. "Promiscuous," "abnormal" or "bizarre" become irrelevant labels for behavior in a culture where all that is needed is an urge to do something and a desire to enjoy it. Hippies rightly summed up their hedonistic philosophy with the expression: "If it feels good, do it!"

The hippie and student movements were the radical standard-bearers of this lifestyle and philosophy. When the explosion of the sixties subsided, the hippie communes and student radicals gradually faded away, but their influence pervaded society. The bizarre fashions and the informal cohabitation of couples that so shocked society then are hardly contested today.[6]

Thus, the sexual liberation movement all but destroyed the sense of modesty—which protects chastity—and seriously eroded both marriage and the family.

NEW STANDARD-BEARERS FOR THE SEXUAL REVOLUTION

The ongoing homosexual offensive is on the cutting edge of the sexual revolution today. Homosexual activists are the new standard-bearers who prepare society to accept and follow ever more promiscuous and abnormal forms of behavior.

To fight this new revolution effectively, one must clearly see the link between the sexual and homosexual revolutions.

To counter the homosexual offensive without also combating the sexual revolution is to disregard a most important part of this battle. Thus, we must struggle all the more against abortion, pornography and promiscuity. We must wage a spiritual crusade to bring chastity back to society and to restore modesty as the necessary guardian of purity and the expression of human dignity and honor.

---

6. To better understand this process of slow assimilation by society, see Plinio Corrêa de Oliveira, *Revolution and Counter-Revolution* (York, Penn.: The American Society for the Defense of Tradition, Family and Property, 2003), pp. 31-32, 96-98. Available at www.tfp.org/what_we_think/rcronline.html.

CHAPTER 3
Origins of the Homosexual Movement:
The Strange Case of Harry Hay

On October 25, 2002, *The New York Times* published a 1,225-word obituary titled "Harry Hay, Early Proponent of Gay Rights, Dies at 90." Why such a long eulogy in one of the nation's most prestigious newspapers?

Harry Hay was among the first to organize American homosexuals into a movement with a defined ideology and goals. His 1950 founding of the Mattachine Society "proved to be the catalyst for the American gay rights movement."[1]

A look at his life is a glimpse below the surface of the homosexual movement.

THE "SILENT BROTHERHOOD"

Stuart Timmons wrote Harry Hay's biography, *The Trouble with Harry Hay*. He tells the story of how Hay became a homosexual and promoted the homosexual revolution.[2]

Timmons narrates Harry Hay's "initiation" into the underworld of homosexuality as a 14-year-old aboard a tramp steamer off the California coast. On this voyage, Hay sought and had homosexual relations with a sailor called Matt, ten years his senior. This sailor revealed to him the existence of an esoteric world with its own culture and signals for members to recognize each other. Matt explained that should Hay find himself in a strange land, fearful of everything and not knowing anyone or the local language, when least expected, he would come across a pair of open shining eyes looking in his direction. "All of a sudden your

---

1. Dudley Clendinen, "Harry Hay, Early Proponent of Gay Rights, Dies at 90," *The New York Times*, Oct. 25, 2002.
2. Stuart Timmons, *The Trouble with Harry Hay* (Boston: Alyson Publications, 1990). More studious readers who want a more in-depth view are advised to obtain a copy of *The Trouble with Harry Hay*.

eyes lock into that pair of eyes, and...you're home and you're safe."[3]

Hay, born and raised a Catholic, left the Church the following year.

MIXING RED AND LAVENDER IN HOLLYWOOD

After dropping out of college, Hay went to Hollywood to try his hand as an actor. He made friends with movie director George Oppenheimer, who introduced him to the homosexual network in the movie capital.[4]

Communism was also making deep inroads into artistic circles. Will Geer, the actor who played Grandpa in *The Waltons*, introduced Hay to the party. This was a milestone in Hay's life. Communism marked Hay's thinking indelibly.[5] He saw how he could apply Marxist dialectics to his own theories about homosexuality.[6]

He joined the party with a religious fervor, which he compared to "joining the Holy Orders in earlier centuries,"[7] and, shortly after, married Anita Platky, a Communist comrade.

ORGANIST AT OCCULTIST CEREMONIES

Around this time, Hay was also playing the organ at "Gnostic Catholic Masses," occultist rituals that were held at the Los Angeles lodge of the Order of the Eastern Temple. The principle mentor of this esoteric society was Aleister

---

3. Hay's Oct. 7, 1984 speech at NAMBLA's San Francisco conference, www.nambla1.de/sanfrancisco1984.htm. Cf. Hay's Feb. 22, 1983 speech at New York University, www.nambla1.de/nyu1983.htm and Timmons, *The Trouble with Harry Hay*, p. 36.
4. Timmons, *The Trouble with Harry Hay*, p. 70.
5. Anne-Marie Cusac, "Hary Hay Interview," www.progressive.org/nov02/hay-intv02.html.
6. Cf. Stuart Timmons, "He Paved the Way for Modern Gay Activism: Harry Hay Dies at 90," *CounterPunch*, Oct. 25, 2002, www.counterpunch.org/timmons1025.html.
7. Timmons, *The Trouble with Harry Hay*, p. 97.

Crowley, the notorious satanist involved in "sexual-religious mysteries."[8]

A MARXIST MOLD TO
CAST THE HOMOSEXUAL REVOLUTION

In 1948, Hay formulated the principles and theories that would give rise to the Mattachine Society two years later. Applying Marxist dialectics to the homosexual cause, he developed the theory that homosexuals were a "cultural minority" oppressed by the dominant heterosexual majority.[9] This concept was key in selling the homosexual movement to the public. As Timmons observes, "This concept of homosexuals as a minority would be the contribution of which Hay was the proudest."[10]

With Hay's strategic concept, old prejudices were buried under new labels.[11] Using this tactic delivered results on two fronts: The aversion of many sentimental people for homosexuals began to diminish, and the number of allies multiplied, since leftists in the media, academia and religion began to regard them as one more "minority" to promote.

THE MATTACHINE SOCIETY:
THE MOVEMENT IS BORN

In 1950, Hay had an affair with the young leftist political

---

8. Martin P. Starr, *The Unknown God: W.T. Smith and the Thelemites* (Bolingbrook, Ill.: The Teitan Press, Inc., 2003), p. 70. Cf. ibid., p. 193, fn. 31, Timmons, *The Trouble with Harry Hay*, p. 75 and "Aleister Crowley: A Legacy of Satanism," www.gothicpress.freeserve.co.uk/Aleister%20Crowley.htm.

9. Cf. ibid., pp. 136, 150-151; Clendinen; "Harry and the Mattachine Society," www.harryhay.com /AH_matt.html.

10. Timmons, *The Trouble with Harry Hay*, p. 136.

11. For a thorough analysis of a similar Communist strategy to effect ideological change, see Plinio Corrêa de Oliveira, "Unperceived Ideological Transshipment and Dialogue," *Crusade for a Christian Civilization*, no. 4, 1982. Also available at www.tfp.org/what_we_think/dialogue/dialogue_chp2.html.

refugee, Rudi Gernreich. The Austrian fashion designer would become famous years later for such women's fashions as the "monokini" swimsuit, topless dresses and see-through clothes. Gernreich also introduced androgyny into fashions, fitting men's suits and hats on women.

With Gernreich's help, Hay recruited the Mattachine Society's first members. The society's first seven members were either Communist Party members or leftist "fellow travelers." The name was taken from a secret male group of masked satirical French dancers during the late Middle Ages.[12]

The Mattachine Society was "unarguably the beginning of the modern gay movement."[13] Its "Missions and Purposes" were "TO UNIFY...TO EDUCATE...TO LEAD...the whole mass of social deviates."[14]

Harry Hay led the discussion inside the society to find a new, more "positive" and "acceptable" term to replace the word "homosexual" which he believed had acquired a pathological, negative connotation. After much debate, they decided to adopt the term *homophile* ("love for the same").[15]

HAY DIVORCES AND
LEAVES THE COMMUNIST PARTY

Though Harry Hay was married for thirteen years and had two adopted daughters, he never gave up homosexuality. Throughout his marriage, he roamed city parks looking for

12. According to some, the name comes from a "French medieval and Renaissance Société Mattachine, a musical masque group.... The name was meant to symbolize the fact that 'gays were a masked people, unknown and anonymous.'" ("Mattachine Society," The Knitting Circle—Lesbian and Gay Staff Association, www.myweb.lsbu.ac.uk/~stafflag/mattachine.html.) See also, Timmons, *The Trouble with Harry Hay*, p. 130.
13. Stuart Timmons, July 13, 2001, interview on "Subversity" with host Daniel C. Tsang, (KUCI, 88.9 fm), www.kuci.uci.edu/~dtsang/subversity/Sv010713.ram.
14. Quoted in Timmons, *The Trouble with Harry Hay*, p. 154.
15. Cf. ibid., pp. 148-149.

homosexual adventures and had many partners until his divorce in 1951.

In that same year, Hay recommended to Party officials that they expel him from membership because of his homosexuality. His membership was terminated, but in acknowledgment of his many dedicated years, the party would ever remember him as "a lifelong friend of the people."[16]

HAY'S EXPULSION FROM THE MATTACHINE SOCIETY

The Mattachine Society continued to develop, and established chapters throughout the country. However, not all members shared the Marxist ideology of its founders. This caused problems for the society during the anti-Communist campaigns of the "McCarthy era."

In February 1953, an article in the Los Angeles press identified Harry Hay as a Marxist teacher. This alarmed some Mattachine members. They found a Communist link to their organization to be unacceptable. An internal crisis developed, and, after much discussion and tension, the group's founders were forced to resign.[17]

CONTINUED COMMUNIST AND HOMOSEXUAL ACTIVISM

Estrangement from the Communist Party and the Mattachine Society did not mean that Harry Hay ceased being

---

16. Cf. Paul Varnell, "Harry Hay: One Big Idea," *Chicago Free Press*, Oct. 30, 2002, www.indegayforum.org/authors/varnell/100.html and Timmons, *The Trouble with Harry Hay*, p. 160.

17. Cf. Jack Nichols, "Hal Call, a Mattachine Society Pioneer—Dead at 83," http://gaytoday.badpuppy.com/garchive/events/122000ev.html; Timmons, *The Trouble with Harry Hay*, p. 179; "Mattachine Society," www.members.aol. com/matrixwerx/ glbthistory/mattachine.htm; "Hope Along the Wind—Harry and the Mattachine Society," www.harryhay.com/AH_matt.html; "Mattachine Society," The Knitting Circle.

a Communist and homosexual activist.

Hay remained very active in the homosexual movement, which grew vastly with the sexual revolution of the sixties and particularly after the 1969 Stonewall Riots. Along with other experienced activists, Harry Hay joined Gay Liberation. One of his fellow members was Morris Kight, an activist who opposed the Vietnam War. In 1969, Harry Hay helped found the Southern California Gay Liberation Front and was its first elected chair.[18]

NAMBLA FRIEND

Although not a member, Harry Hay was an admirer of the North American Man/Boy Love Association—NAMBLA, founded in Boston in 1978.[19] He spoke frequently at NAMBLA events and came to the defense of this organization when other homosexual groups tried to prevent it from joining Gay Pride parades.[20] He advocated homosexual relations between men and boys. Citing his own case—when he was 9, 11, and 12 years of age—he said he honored the men who looked for him then "and who gave me the opportunity to learn love and trust at a very early age."[21]

HAY FOUNDS THE HOMOSEXUAL
NEOPAGAN RADICAL FAERIES

In 1979, Hay founded Radical Faeries, a mystical, neo-pagan homosexual movement which today has spread to many other countries.

---

18. Cf. Timmons, *The Trouble with Harry Hay*, pp. 229-230.
19. "Harry was a vocal and courageous supporter of NAMBLA and intergenerational sexual relationships…. I first met Harry in early 1983, at the time of the first of these speeches. I was introduced to him…by lesbian activist, self-professed witch, and sometime weed partner Katherine Davenport, a mutual friend." David Thorstad, "Harry Hay on Man/Boy Love," www.nambla1.de/losangeles1986.htm.
20. Cf. www.nambla1.de/hayonmanboylove.htm. Also, Timmons's book shows pictures of Hay wearing a poncho with the saying: "NAMBLA Walks With Me."
21. www.nambla1.de/sanfrancisco1984.htm.

CHAPTER 4
The Homosexual Network: Spinning a Web

Applying the words of Prof. Plinio Corrêa de Oliveira, to think that the homosexual revolution reached its present state without some kind of organization or coordination is like believing that hundreds of Scrabble letters thrown out a window could arrange themselves spontaneously on the ground so as to spell out a literary piece, such as Carducci's "Ode to Satan."[1]

FROM *BOWERS* TO *LAWRENCE*

In 1986, the Supreme Court delivered a resounding no to sodomy in its *Bowers v. Hardwick* decision. A mere 17 years later, in *Lawrence v. Texas*, the same court reversed *Bowers* and granted constitutional protection to sodomy.

In an August 3 article in *The Boston Globe*, titled "Rainbow Warriors," Laura Secor analyzes how this reversal came about. After *Bowers*, the homosexual movement mobilized and counterattacked. Not much was left to chance. Its influence in academia, the media and the entertainment world was fully mustered. Lobbying in state legislatures and activism in the courts succeeded in overturning laws against sodomy in 12 of the 25 states where they existed.

All of these factors contributed to the homosexual move-ment's decisive role in 2003's two landmark cases: *Lawrence v. Texas* and *Goodridge v. Department of Public Health* in Massachusetts.

THE HOMOSEXUAL NETWORK

Although homosexuals constitute a minority of less than three percent of the population,[2] the movement is highly

---

1. Cf. Plinio Corrêa de Oliveira, *Revolution and Counter-Revolution*, p. 38.
2. Cf. Edward O. Laumann, et al., *The Social Organization of Sexuality* (Chicago: The University of Chicago Press, 1994), p. 293.

organized and well financed.

In his 1982 book *The Homosexual Network*, Fr. Enrique T. Rueda listed more than a hundred organizations that were part of the homosexual movement at that time.[3] Thirteen years later, in 1995, Dr. Charles W. Socarides wrote: "I have heard estimates as high as 14,000 individual chapters for various national and regional gay and lesbian associations."[4] This shows a staggering organizational structure and expansion.

Space does not allow the listing of all the associations, groups, web sites and publications that constitute the homosexual movement. Instead, a broad outline is provided which will show the main channels it uses to influence society. Only a few organizations are mentioned as examples.

INTERNATIONAL SCOPE

The homosexual movement in the United States is energized by the fact that the homosexual revolution is a worldwide phenomenon.

The International Association of Lesbian, Gay, Bisexual, Transgendered Pride Coordinators, Inc. (InterPride) works on the international plane, encouraging and assisting homosexual parades around the world. From New York to Sydney, São Paulo to Vienna, Los Angeles to Johannesburg, InterPride networks with local organizations and helps them with their parades. Its 2003 "Global Pride Calendar" lists parades planned in 26 countries. Sixty delegations from 15 countries attended its 2000 conference. InterPride claims a combined attendance of over 15 million at Gay Pride parades it patronized.[5]

---

3. Fr. Enrique T. Rueda, *The Homosexual Network: Private Lives and Public Policy* (Old Greenwich, Conn.: The Devin Adair Company, 1982).
4. Charles W. Socarides, *Homosexuality—A Freedom Too Far* (Phoenix: Adam Margrave Books, 1995), p. 287.
5. www.interpride.org/mission.htm.

InterPride's anti-Catholic views were made clear during the Church's Jubilee Holy Year in 2000:

> In response both to the Vatican's Millennium 2000 campaign and to widespread discrimination against the GLBT community in Italy, InterPride licensed the first World Pride title to Rome, Italy. This first World Pride, organized and produced by Circolo Mario Mieli in Rome with support and assistance by InterPride, took place in July 2000, and culminated in an international Pride March of over 700,000 through the streets of Rome.[6]

INFLUENCING POLITICS AND LEGISLATION

Among homosexual organizations focused on the political and legislative worlds, two stand out as major players: the National Gay and Lesbian Task Force and Human Rights Campaign.

- **National Gay and Lesbian Task Force**

The goal of the National Gay and Lesbian Task Force (NGLTF) is to build a "powerful political movement" through voter mobilization and training, organizing activists and networking with "oppressed minorities" involved in "gay liberation." The organization "is committed to building a progressive GLBT political infrastructure."[7] To intervene in legislative matters, NGLTF tracks issues of interest to the homosexual movement in state legislatures and drafts proposed legislation. It has been very active over the last 30 years. One of its most important accomplishments was having successfully lobbied the American Psychiatric Association to

---

6. Ibid.
7. www.ngltf.org/about/work.htm.

remove homosexuality from the list of psychiatric disorders in its *Diagnosis and Statistical Manual* (DSM—III) in 1973.[8]

• Human Rights Campaign

Human Rights Campaign (HRC) was founded in 1980 as a political action committee to help elect homosexual congressional candidates and those favorable to the movement.[9] In addition to promoting marches and demonstrations in Washington, HRC actively participates in state, congressional and presidential campaigns. Thus, in 2002 HRC gave $1.2 million in political campaign contributions. Eighty-five percent of the candidates it supported—196 politicians—won their races and will most likely support some parts of the homosexual agenda.

In 1992, HRC endorsed Bill Clinton for president. HRC's web site states, "gay and lesbian voters contributed $3 million to Clinton's campaign and voted in a bloc for the first time, giving him his 5 percent margin of victory."

USING LITIGATION TO EFFECT SOCIAL CHANGE

The Lambda Legal Defense and Education Fund (Lambda Legal) provides legal advice and helps homosexuals who have cases at all levels of the court system throughout the country. The organization focuses on "test cases" that can have far-reaching effects.

Lawrence v. Texas is a prime example. Lambda Legal turned a common police case—the arrest of John Lawrence and Tyron Garner for the crime of sodomy—into a cause célèbre, appealing the case until it reached the Supreme Court. Lambda Legal's supervising attorney, Susan Sommer, rejoiced at its victory: "Even beyond what we can do with it technically as a legal

---

8. Cf. www.ngltf.org/about/highlights.htm. NGLTF's list of activities spans many printed pages.
9. Information gathered from their web site: www.hrc.org.

precedent, which is quite a bit, it also simply changes the land-scape, **changes the culture**, and reflects an enormous shift in this nation."[10]

INFLUENCING THE MEDIA

The Gay & Lesbian Alliance Against Defamation (GLAAD) lobbies the news and entertainment media, aiming to influence public opinion. GLAAD's executive director, Joan Garry, says that the organization's role is "changing people's hearts and minds through what they see in the media."[11]

Among its victories, GLAAD lists *The New York Times*'s change in its editorial policy to replace the word "homosexual" with "gay" in 1987, as well as its 2002 decision to join 140 newspapers across the country in publishing homosexual unions as wedding or celebration announcements.[12] GLAAD also protested Marriage Protection Week 2003, which, in the words of GLAAD's communication director, is really an "attack on our gay and lesbian friends."[13]

INFLUENCING EDUCATION

At a time when the youth are forming their character, good and bad influences can have lasting effect. Regrettably, the homosexual movement has an undeniable influence in schools and universities.

The National Consortium of Directors of Lesbian Gay Bisexual and Transgender Resources in Higher Education provides advice and help to anyone who wants to start a GLBT resource center on campus. Campus PrideNet is another organization that provides resources, advice and ideas to local homosexual activists and groups. Other

---

10. www.lambdalegal.org/cgi-bin/iowa/documents/recor?record+1283. (Our emphasis.)
11. www.glaad.org/about/index.php.
12. www.glaad.org/about/history.php.
13. www.glaad.org/publications/op-ed_detail.php?id=3515.

organizations specialize in coordinating teachers' associations on campuses nationwide.[14]

Google's web directory for gay, lesbian and bisexual student organizations lists 196 groups across the country.[15] Most college campuses in the country, even Catholic ones, have a GLBT or similar homosexual group.[16]

INFLUENCING RELIGION

Every major religion has an association that promotes the acceptance of homosexuality.[17] Unfortunately, activists misrepresent even the Catholic Church's unchangeable moral teaching on homosexuality.

Soulforce defines itself as "an interfaith movement committed to ending spiritual violence perpetuated by religious policies and teachings against gay, lesbian, bisexual, and transgendered people."[18] It defines its primary goal as follows:

> We believe that religion has become the primary source of false and inflammatory misinformation about lesbian, gay, bisexual, and transgendered people. Fundamentalist Christians teach that we are "sick" and "sinful." Liberal Christian denominations teach that we are "incompatible with Christian teaching." Most conservative and liberal denominations

---

14. These include the American Federation of Teachers/National Gay and Lesbian Caucus; the Gay, Lesbian, and Straight Teachers Network; the National Educational Association's Gay and Lesbian Caucus; and Teachers Group: Gays and Lesbians Working in Education.

15. http://directory.google.com/Top/Society/Gay,_Lesbian,_and_Bisexual/ Student/Colleges_and_Universities/North_America/United_States/.

16. Cf. www3.villanova.edu/bglov/ and www-acc.scu.edu/clubs/GALA/home-page.html.

17. Cf. www.dv-8.com/resources/us/national/religious.html. This web site links to homosexual resources around the world. Under US National Religious GLBT Organizations there are 35 listings.

18. www.soulforce.org/main/mission/shtml.

refuse to marry us or ordain us for ministry. The
Roman Catholic Church teaches that our orientation
is "objectively disordered" and our acts of intimacy
"intrinsically evil." They teach that we should not
marry, adopt, co-parent, teach children, coach youth
or serve in the military. Members of Dignity (the
Catholic GLBT organization) are refused the use of
Church property and the presence of a priest to conduct a Dignity Mass. We believe these teachings lead
to discrimination, suffering and death. Our goal is to
confront and eventually replace these tragic untruths
with the truth that we are God's children, too, created,
loved, and accepted by God exactly as we are.[19]

A sampling of specifically Catholic dissident organizations
promoting the acceptance of homosexuality within the
Catholic Church includes Dignity/USA,[20] New Ways Ministry,
Call to Action, the Conference of Catholic Lesbians, Inc. and
the Rainbow Sash Movement.

19. www.soulforce.org/main/faq.shtml.
20. On July 29, 2003, Dignity published a communiqué titled "Gay Catholics Reject
    Vatican Document on Same-Sex Marriage," denying Catholic doctrine on
    homosexuality. www.dignityusa.org/datelines/dl2003/oct03dl.html.

Georgetown: Two Examples
of Liberal Tolerance

Liberal tolerance finds ways to protect and favor evil, while leaving good to its own devices or obstructing it altogether. This liberal tolerance manifested itself recently in two episodes at America's oldest Catholic university.

*   *   *

On May 17, 2003, Francis Cardinal Arinze, prefect of the Congregation for Divine Worship and the Discipline of the Sacraments, delivered the address at the graduation ceremonies. He stated:

> In many parts of the world, the family is under siege. It is opposed by an anti-life mentality as is seen in contraception, abortion, infanticide and euthanasia. It is scorned and banalized by pornography, desecrated by fornication and adultery, mocked by homosexuality, sabotaged by irregular unions and cut in two by divorce.[21]

Part of the audience was quite upset with the reference to homosexuality. Students walked out and a theology professor stomped off the stage. Later, an official letter of protest was signed by nearly seventy faculty members.

*   *   *

In October, young members of TFP Student Action–carrying the American flag, the TFP's large red standard with the golden lion, playing bagpipes and wearing their trademark red capes–started campaigns on college campuses.

---

21. Nick Timiraos, "Cardinal's Commencement Remarks Spark Controversy," *The Hoya*, June 3, 2003.

They collected signatures protesting the Supreme Court's *Lawrence v. Texas* decision legalizing sodomy and handed out copies of "Are We Still 'One Nation Under God'?" the TFP statement on this landmark decision (see Appendix).

On November 20, 2003, they visited Georgetown, the first Catholic campus on their circuit. The reaction they encountered surprised them.

Though merely reaffirming natural law and the most recent Church teaching on homosexuality, a university official deemed the handout "grossly offensive." Security guards confronted two TFP members campaigning on Red Square–the official "free speech zone"–and escorted them off campus with a warning that, if they returned, they would be arrested.

The TFP's short campaign caused an uproar. In a broadcast e-mail on November 25, Todd Olson, Interim Vice President for Student Affairs, explained that he ordered the TFP members removed because there is a difference between "free" and "offensive" speech. For him, the TFP flier was "grossly offensive and inflammatory." He also noted that "intolerance and invective have no place at Georgetown."

However, Olson's message to campus homosexuals had another tone:

> I would like to take this opportunity to emphasize that gay, lesbian, bisexual, and transgender members of our community enjoy the right to study, work and live in a campus environment of respect and protection.[22]

---

22. Cf. Shanthi Manian, "Free Speech But Not Hate Speech," *Georgetown Voice*, Dec. 4, 2003; Aaron Terrazas "Anti-Gay Protester Removed From Red Square for 'Offensive Speech,'" *The Hoya*, Dec. 5, 2003; Paul Weyrich, "Christian Values Unwelcome," *Washington Dispatch*, Dec. 17, 2003; Jim Brown, "Group Protesting Sodomy Ruling Ejected From Georgetown Campus," *AgapePress*, Dec. 30, 2003.

The administration's publicized defense of its harsh
measures, the news reports in campus publications and the
ensuing letters to the editor generated nationwide interest.
Articles in conservative publications and postings on web
sites and bulletin boards questioned the integrity of the
Catholic Faith at the prestigious institution. Many associated
the TFP's expulsion with the furor that followed Cardinal
Arinze's speech six months earlier.

*   *   *

It is troubling indeed to see a Catholic university show
such intolerance for Church authority and moral teaching. It
is nevertheless a sad illustration of the inroads made by the
homosexual movement in Catholic schools and universities.

CHAPTER 5
Exposing the Movement's Tactics:
You Are the Target

In 1989 two Harvard-educated homosexuals, Marshall Kirk, a researcher in neuropsychiatry, and Hunter Madsen, an expert in public persuasion tactics and social marketing, wrote *After the Ball: How America Will Conquer Its Fear & Hatred of Gays in the 90s.*

The authors declare in the acknowledgements that they were approached by editor Marshall DeBruhl and asked to write a "gay manifesto for the 1990s." The result was *After the Ball*, a veritable blueprint for marketing the homosexual cultural revolution in America.

The authors sought to outline ways to change how America looks upon homosexuality. Lasting change only comes when people are persuaded. Kirk and Madsen argued that the homosexual movement's tactics were not persuasive and showed how this could be reversed. *After the Ball* advocates a major change in tactics: "The campaign we outline in this book, though complex, depends centrally upon a program of unabashed propaganda, firmly grounded in long established principles of psychology and advertising."[1]

SHEDDING AN UGLY IMAGE

When the book was written, the homosexual movement was in crisis. The sexual liberation explosion of the sixties and seventies was over and AIDS had made devastating advances. Above all, public perception was decidedly negative. Kirk and Madsen concluded this was due in part to the promiscuous and shockingly vulgar public behavior of some elements in

---

1. Marshall Kirk and Hunter Madsen, *After the Ball: How America Will Conquer its Fear & Hatred for Gays in the 90s* (New York: Penguin Books USA, Inc., 1990), p. xxviii. More studious readers who want a more in-depth view are advised to obtain a copy of *After the Ball*.

the movement. Some reasons they listed for this negative image were:

- The transformation of public restrooms (including men's rooms at Ivy League colleges), parks and alleyways into homosexual "brothels;"
- Homosexual and lesbian transvestites riding powerful motorcycles in homosexual parades;
- Participation in these parades by organizations such as the North American Man/Boy Love Association (NAMBLA);
- The pervasive sadomasochism and rivalries in homosexual bars and bathhouses.[2]

The authors insisted that image-management is vital for success. They called upon the homosexual movement to "clean up its act" and discard everything that contributed to this negative image. Perception is everything in this cultural war, and, to win, homosexuals must *look* good.

DIFFERENT SCRIPTS FOR DIFFERENT AUDIENCES

The authors recommended that homosexual activists use different scripts for different audiences. Any script, however, must speak to the heart, not the head. The focus should be on manipulating the public's emotions, not addressing it with logical arguments.[3]

Kirk and Madsen divided the American public into three roughly equal groups and recommend corresponding tactics:

1) those *vehemently opposed* to homosexuality—**isolate and silence**;
2) the *undecided Middle America*—**desensitize, jam and convert**;

---

2. Cf. ibid., pp. 306-313.
3. Cf. ibid., p. 162.

3) those *friendly* to the homosexual movement—
mobilize.[4]

The movement's psychological attack should be carried out simultaneously on all three fronts, since results on each front are compounded by the combined effort.

THE MOST IMPORTANT:
DESENSITIZE, JAM AND CONVERT

Kirk and Madsen claimed that the most vital group to be targeted was undecided Middle America, or, in their description, "the ambivalent skeptics." They explain the tactics to be used with this crucial sector of the public:

> Desensitization aims at lowering the intensity of antigay emotional reactions to a level approximating sheer indifference; Jamming attempts to blockade or counteract the rewarding "pride in prejudice"...by attaching to homohatred a pre-existing, and punishing, sense of shame in being a bigot.... Both Desensitization and Jamming...are mere preludes to our highest—though necessarily very long-range—goal, which is Conversion. It isn't enough that antigay bigots should become confused about us, or even indifferent to us—we are safest, in the long run, if we can actually make them like us. Conversion aims at just this....
>
> By Conversion we actually mean something far more profoundly threatening to the American Way of Life, without which no truly sweeping social change can occur. We mean conversion of the average American's emotions, mind, and will, through a

---

4. Cf. ibid., pp. 175-177.

planned psychological attack, in the form of propaganda fed to the nation via the media.[5]

GOING ON THE OFFENSIVE

Kirk and Madsen provided many suggestions of how to carry out this three-pronged propaganda war on the American Way of Life. Some of the tactics for each of these three groups are:

1) For friends and allies of the homosexual movement:

- Encourage the largest possible number of homosexuals and lesbians from all walks of life and professions, especially celebrities, to "come out." This creates insecurity in the public's rejection of homosexuality.[6]
- Focus much more on non-discrimination, human rights and equality. Do not try to defend homosexual behavior or the homosexual lifestyle. Keep the discussion abstract, high up in the clouds of social and philosophical theory.
- Use the AIDS epidemic to demand civil rights for homosexuals, and raise the issue of discrimination.
- Use the media. Carry out media campaigns in conjunction with—prior to is even better—political action drives.
- Network with non-homosexual organizations that are willing to provide moral support for the homosexual cause.
- Always present homosexuals as good.

---

5. Ibid., p. 153.
6. The 1997 TV "coming out" of actress Ellen Degeneres is an example of this tactic suggested by Kirk and Madsen.

"Homophobia"—A Semantic Weapon in the Cultural War

Arthur Evans, co-founder of Gay Activists Alliance (GAA), explains how the homosexual movement came up with the word *homophobia* to characterize their opposition:

> By good fortune, George Weinberg, a straight psychologist who had long been a friend of our community, regularly attended GAA meetings. Watching with fascination our zaps and the media responses, he came up with the word we had been struggling for— "homophobia,"…meaning the irrational fear of loving someone of the same sex....
>
> The invention of the word "homophobia" is an example of how theory can be rooted in practice. The word didn't come from an arm-chair academic viewing the movement at a distance.... Instead, it came from personal interactions among active, thinking people who acknowledged a shared value: **the transformation of society for the better**.[7]

George Weinberg thus classified moral opposition to homosexuality as a phobia: "I would never consider a patient healthy unless he had overcome his prejudice against homosexuality."[8]

Weinberg's rationale has inevitable religious consequences: A sexual morality in accordance with natural law and the

---

7. Arthur Evans, "The Logic of Homophobia," http://gaytoday.badpuppy.com/garchive/viewpoint/101600vi.htm. (Our emphasis.)
8. Quoted in Jack Nichols, "George Weinberg, Ph.D.—Badpuppy's February Interview," http://gaytoday.badpuppy.com/garchive/interview/020397in.htm.

moral teachings of the Catholic Church is harmful since it engenders prejudice and irrational fears.

The homosexual movement employs words and concepts as semantic weapons to change individuals and society. Concepts like compassion are meant to build acceptance, while others, like homophobia, are meant to inhibit and even paralyze reactions.

By affixing the homophobic label to its opponents, the movement hopes to both intimidate and disqualify its antagonists, brushing off their arguments based on right reason as "irrational fears."

Those who defend natural law and the Ten Commandments should scorn this dishonest tactic. They should challenge the demagogical use of the homophobe label by asking for the **scientific** proofs for this so-called phobia, "discovered" by an activist intent on pushing the homosexual agenda.

2) For those vehemently opposed to homosexuality:

- Demonize anti-homosexuals. Paint them as evil as possible so that the general public feels uncomfortable in their presence and avoids them. Label them Klansmen, Nazis, racists, anti-Semites or unbalanced freaks.
- For example, use the "bracket technique" to demonize anti-homosexuals and portray homosexuals as victims. In other words, develop commercials that show, for example, the fire-and-brimstone sermons of Southern preachers consigning homosexuals to Hell. Contrast this rhetoric with images of decent, ordinary-looking, but badly mistreated homosexual victims.[9]
- Present conservative and traditional church doctrine as

9. Kirk and Madsen, pp. 189-190.

fossilized and out of step with breakthroughs in
science, particularly in the realm of psychology.

3) For undecided Middle America:

- Homosexuals must be portrayed as victims of circumstance who stand in need of protection. The public
  must be brought around psychologically to feeling it
  must extend this protection to homosexuals in order to
  be consistent with its own principles.
- Present homosexuals as people who are born that way
  and who cannot change even if they so wished. This
  leaves the public psychologically torn on how to act
  towards homosexuals: If it is not their fault, how can
  homosexuals be blamed?
- In TV commercials, do not trot out masculine women,
  drag queens and so on. Instead, present the most
  ordinary-looking people: Show images of youngsters,
  middle-aged women, older people who are parents and
  friends of homosexuals.
- More than public acts of self-affirmation, homosexual
  parades should aim to *communicate* with the public.
  They should be marches, not parades. Do not impose
  homosexuality on the public. Rather, help the public to
  understand homosexuals.
- Avoid shocking the public by prematurely exposing
  homosexual behavior.
- Weaken religious opposition to homosexuality by
  obscuring the waters. Divide and conquer. Cast liberal
  and moderate churches against conservative ones.
- Stay on message: Talk everywhere, all the time, only
  about homosexuality, in a neutral tone, until the public
  is saturated. Once saturated, the public stops paying

attention. It has become calloused and numb to the issue. Win by exhaustion.

- Educating the public is more important than securing short-term victories with the help of liberal elites in government. Unless the public is persuaded (or numbed into indifference), all gains are ephemeral.

- Use celebrities to endorse the homosexual lifestyle. They do not have to be homosexuals themselves, all that is expected of them is to give homosexuality their celebrity stamp of approval.[10]

- In the propaganda campaign's initial stages, use lesbians as the poster girls, not homosexuals. The public will be more receptive. Men are perceived as being more of a menace.

- Present great historic personages as homosexuals. Dead historic figures will not sue for damages to their reputation. The idea that homosexuality is associated with greatness, however, shakes people's beliefs.

Kirk and Madsen concluded that the final outcome of this enormous propaganda war would be the acceptance of homosexuality, if not directly as "good," at least as a tolerable variant of normality.

THE FACTS CONFIRM THE TACTICS

Kirk and Madsen's book stirred up a debate. Some homosexual activists downplayed its importance. Others attempted to discredit its straightforward approach. More radical homosexuals saw its call to "moderation" as a sell-out to heterosexual society.[11]

Such debate skirts the main issue. It matters little if homosexual activists viewed *After the Ball* as their bedside book,

---

10. We believe the August 2003 voluptuous kiss between Madonna, Britney Spears and Cristina Aguillera at an MTV Award ceremony is an example of this celebrity endorsement for the homosexual lifestyle.

11. Cf. Steve Miller, "Culture Watch," Independent Gay Forum, May 24, 2002, www.indegayforum.org/culturewatch/2002_05_19_archive.shtml.

meditating on it daily, or if they minimized its importance. What does matter is that the homosexual movement by and large adopted many of the strategies and tactics suggested by its authors. Indeed, if a book were written describing the tactics employed by homosexual organizations since 1989, it would have much in common with the Kirk and Madsen blueprint.

Additionally, *After the Ball* is important because it makes it very clear that the homosexual revolution is waging a propaganda war, describes its strategy and tactics and identifies Christian Middle America as its target.

PERSUASION IS THE KEY

Marketing specialist Paul E. Rondeau analyzed Kirk and Madsen's book in his study "Selling Homosexuality to America," and focused on the vital role of persuasion in the cultural war to change America's position on homosexuality:

> Among America's culture wars, one of today's most intense controversies rages around the issue alternatively identified, depending on one's point of view, as "normalizing homosexuality" or "accepting gayness." The debate is truly a social-ethical-moral conceptual war that transcends both the scientific and legal, though science and law most often are the weapon of choice. The ammunition of these weapons, however, is persuasion.[12]

Victory in this Cultural War will go to the camp that can bring or keep American public opinion on its side. Kirk and Madsen perceived this very well. Americans who seek to uphold the traditional family must also be convinced of this reality.

---

12. Paul E. Rondeau, "Selling Homosexuality to America," *Regent University Law Review*, 2002, Vol. 14, p. 443. Available at www.regent.edu/acad/schlaw/lawreview/articles/14_2Rondeau.pdf.

The Ten Percent Myth

The ten percent myth was based on research done by zoologist and taxonomy expert Alfred C. Kinsey, and published in his 1948 study, *Sexual Behavior in the Human Male* (commonly known as the Kinsey Report).

Among the conclusions found in the Kinsey Report is the idea that ten percent of males are more or less exclusively homosexual and four percent of white males are exclusively homosexual throughout their lives.

The Kinsey Report was proven to be flawed. Kinsey's sample of 5,300 men, for example, "included several hundred prostitutes, 1,200 convicted sex offenders, high numbers of pedophiles and exhibitionists, and a quarter of his sample were prison inmates, who are disproportionately homosexual." [13]

Research by Edward O. Laumann and others debunked Kinsey's ten percent figures, finding Kinsey's figures much higher than those in population surveys. Laumann's conclusion was that "2.8 percent of the men and 1.4 percent of the women reported some level of homosexual (bisexual) identity."[14]

Laumann noted that, despite such evidence, the homosexual movement made use of the ten percent myth for its propaganda war. He notes that Bruce Voeller, the founder of the National Gay and Lesbian Task Force, claims to have launched the use of the ten percent estimate as part of its campaign in the late 1970s to convince politicians and

---

13. A. Dean Byrd and Stony Olsen, "Homosexuality: Innate and Immutable?" *Regent University Law Review*, Vol. 14:513, p. 546.
14. Laumann, p. 289.

the public that homosexuals were everywhere.[15]

Recently, the homosexual movement itself abandoned the ten percent myth. According to Ed Vitagliano, a coalition of 31 homosexual advocacy groups, including the Human Rights Campaign, the National Gay and Lesbian Task Force, and the Gay and Lesbian Alliance Against Defamation, filed a brief in *Lawrence v. Texas*, in which the coalition used Laumann's figures, that only "2.8% of the male, and 1.4% of the female population identify themselves as gay, lesbian, or bisexual."[16]

---

15. Cf. ibid..
16. "Homosexual Advocacy Groups Admit 10% Fallacy," *Agape Press*, Jul. 30, 2003, http://headlines.agapepress.org/archive/7/302003e.asp.

CHAPTER 6

Why Same-Sex "Marriage" Matters: Validating the Homosexual Ideology

Media reports following the Supreme Court ruling on *Lawrence v. Texas* focused on the next milestone in the homosexual agenda: same-sex "marriage." The title of a *Newsweek* cover story, for example, stated: "Is Gay Marriage Next?" The CBS News web site simply announced, "The Next Battle: Gay Marriage."

Same-sex "marriage" was a hot topic at Gay Pride parades in New York and San Francisco on June 29, 2003. In New York, sixty homosexual couples were symbolically united in a mock wedding ceremony before the parade began.[1]

Laura Secor of *The Boston Globe* observed that "at the moment same-sex marriage is the most high-profile, and potentially polarizing, gay-rights issue on the nation's political agenda."[2]

SAME-SEX "MARRIAGE"— A POWERFUL PSYCHOLOGICAL WEAPON

It seems that contrary to what is normally heard, the homosexual movement's primary goals in seeking the legalization of same-sex "marriage" are not the financial or health benefits associated with marriage. It is not even the search for stability and exclusivity in a homosexual relationship. The principal objective in seeking same-sex "marriage" is to acquire a powerful psychological weapon to change society's rejection of homosexuality into gradual, even if reluctant, acceptance.

If public opinion resists the legalization of same-sex "marriage" proper, the homosexual movement will settle for "civil unions," "domestic partnerships" or any other euphemism.

---

1. Cf. www.nydailynews.com/06-30-2003/news/local/story/96774p-87658c.html.
2. Laura Secor, "Rainbow Warriors."

Unfortunately, many people see the acceptance of such labels as a concession on the part of the movement. They are blind to the fact that the legal and social recognition of these euphemistic labels is the legal and social recognition of homosexual unions per se. Far from being concessions, they are stepping stones that allow the movement to attain its prized goal of same-sex "marriage" in the medium term.

SAME-SEX "MARRIAGE" IS NOT MARRIAGE

Regarding same-sex "marriage," Lambda Legal published this "Marriage Resolution" on its web site:

> Because marriage is a basic human right and an individual personal choice, RESOLVED, the State should not interfere with same-gender couples who choose to marry and share fully and equally in the rights, responsibilities, and commitment of civil marriage.[3]

This resolution accurately sums up the homosexual movement's arguments for same-sex "marriage." However, this resolution is based on a false analogy. It draws a conclusion from an analogy between facts or situations that share an accidental resemblance but are essentially different. This is the resolution's flawed line of reasoning:

1) Marriage is a basic human right;
2) Marriage is an individual personal choice;
3) Therefore, same-gender couples can choose to marry and share fully and equally in the rights, responsibilities and commitment of civil marriage;
4) And the State should not interfere in their decision.

All recognize that marriage is a "basic human right" and a

---

3.   www.lambdalegal.org/cgi-bin/iowa/documents/record?record=143.

"personal choice." Most recognize that it deserves State protection. However, the analogy made in the third sentence between a same-sex couple and the marriage between a man and a woman is false.

As a "basic human right," the right to marriage stems from human nature, and thus its existence precedes both Church and State. Nevertheless, that same human nature which gives rise to this "basic human right" also requires that marriage be the union of man and woman since the cooperation of both is required in accomplishing the primary purpose of marriage, which is the procreation and education of children.[4] The civil "marriage" of two individuals of the same sex is not based on human nature. Therefore, it is not marriage, so there is no "basic human right" to same-sex "marriage."

The fact that marriage is an "individual personal choice" does not mean that *any* type of union between two individuals can be called marriage or that such unions deserve to "share fully and equally in the rights, responsibilities, and commitment of civil marriage." Marriage is more than just a business partnership where the duration and the nature of the contract depend entirely on the will of the parties.

The "individual personal choice" in marriage is exercised both in opting for the marital state and in the choice of one's spouse. However, the future spouses are not free to alter marriage's essential purpose or properties. These do not depend on the will of the contracting parties. They are rooted in natural law and do not change. Natural law, not the spouses, determines the purpose of marriage as well as the number and sex of the contracting parties. The idea that homosexuals can create same-sex "marriage" through their individual choice is false.

Finally, the statement that "the State should not interfere with their decision" is also false. When the State proscribes

---

4. See box on the primary end of marriage in Chapter 9.

the union between two individuals of the same sex, it neither violates the basic human right to marriage nor one's right to freely choose a spouse because this union is not marriage. Moreover, by enacting laws allowing homosexuals to enter into same-sex "marriage," the State would violate its own purpose, which is to assure the common good of society and safeguard public morality.

SENTIMENTALITY IS NOT AN ARGUMENT

As seen before, Kirk and Madsen recommended speaking to the heart, not the head. They suggested manipulating people's emotions, not addressing them with rational logic.

Thus, homosexual organizations use sentimental arguments to justify same-sex "marriage." For example, Marriage Equality USA suggests people remember their own beautiful weddings:

> **What, Exactly, Is Marriage?**
>
> For anyone reading this that is already married, think back to the day your spouse asked you to share his or her life with you. How special your wedding day was! Friends and family gathered around ensuring all was perfect—and for the most part, it was.
>
> Rice and cake aside, had you any idea what marriage meant? Did you know the legal rights you, as husband and wife, would gain? Or how your family was protected?[5]

Regardless of how a false analogy is packaged, one must never forget that packaging does not alter substance. An emotionally packaged false analogy is still a false analogy.

Without same-sex "marriage," the homosexual movement's

---

5. www.marriageequality.org/facts.php?page=what_is_marriage.

bid to impose its ideology on America will fail. The scuttling of the movement's efforts in this regard is vitally important for all Americans who respect and love natural law and the Ten Commandments, and the social order derived from them.

CHAPTER 7
Making the Immoral Moral

In its subversive "moral revolution," the homosexual movement cannot simply jettison all morality, since this would leave a void in the human soul. Homosexuals must convince themselves and society that homosexuality is good and moral. It must create its own pseudo-morality.

Homosexual propaganda does this in several ways. However, all efforts rotate around one central axis of reasoning which can be outlined as follows:

1) I feel sexually attracted to people of my sex;
2) Sexual behavior consistent with this inclination gives me pleasure;
3) Pleasure is good;
4) Therefore, homosexuality is good.

In an article titled "The Virtue of Homosexuality," homosexual writer John Corvino illustrates this ethical justification for homosexuality:

> I have spent my last five columns—and a good deal of my career—defending homosexuality against various moral attacks. Yet sometimes I spend so much time explaining why homosexuality is "not bad" that I neglect to consider why it's positively good. Can I offer any reasons for thinking of homosexuality as, not merely tolerable, but morally beneficial?…
>
> First, homosexuality can be a source of pleasure, and pleasure is a good thing. Too often we act as if pleasure needs to be 'justified' by some extrinsic reason, and we feel guilty when we pursue it for its own sake…. This is not to say that pleasure is the only, or most important, human good. Nor is it to deny that long-term pleasure sometimes requires

short-term sacrifice. But any moral system that doesn't
value pleasure is defective for that reason.[1]

This is *hedonism*, the philosophical system developed by
the Greek philosopher Epicurus that holds pleasure to be the
defining principle of human life. This hedonism confounds
pleasure with goodness ("good" is what causes pleasure), or
subordinates goodness to pleasure. This subverts the whole
moral order and poisons the very fountain of morality.

Once the false premise of hedonistic philosophy is accepted,
an irreversible logic takes over: If pleasure can justify homosexual behavior, then other deviant forms of sexual behavior
deemed pleasurable can also be logically justified. This
includes pedophilia, pederasty, ephebophilia, gerontophilia,
necrophilia, sadism, masochism, bestiality and many other
types of deviant behavior.

FALSE ETHICS PRESUPPOSE A FALSE WORLDVIEW

Man's rational nature compels him to find meaning and
purpose for his life. He may try to flee the profound underlying
philosophical and theological questions of life, but his
rationality always forces him to confront them. As a result,
every individual, whatever his background, ends up establishing
or adopting a philosophy and theology for himself. This
worldview may be rudimentary or even embryonic, but man's
relentless rational nature does not rest until it possesses this
explanation.

In this quest for the meaning of existence, behavior and
ideas influence each other profoundly and seek the consistency
demanded by reason. As Paul Bourget observes in his celebrated work, *Le Demon de Midi*, "One must live as one thinks,

---

1. John Corvino, "The Virtue of Homosexuality," *Between the Lines*, Feb. 7, 2003,
   www.indegayforum.org/authors/corvino/corvino4.html.

under pain, sooner or later, of thinking as one has lived."[2]

The radicalism of the homosexual "moral revolution" leads inevitably to a great clash. This is a clash of two worldviews, a Christian worldview and one that is intrinsically anti-Christian.

2. Paul Bourget, *Le Demon de Midi* (Paris: Librairie Plon, 1914), Vol. 2, p. 375. (Our translation.)

CHAPTER 8
Mystical Eroticism:
The Hidden Side of the Rainbow

Oh! Why should I speak of things unfit to be uttered?
—Athenagoras of Athens

As the homosexual ideology makes inroads into American culture, androgynous trends become ever more noticeable in society. Writing in the *Journal of Sex Research*, Margaret Schneider observes:

> The sexual revolution, which began in the 1960s with the rise of the counterculture and, later, combined with the second wave of feminism, brought a surge of so-called sexual liberation to mainstream North America accompanied by a particular mode of gender-bending. In the interests of mental health and equal opportunity, women were permitted to behave a little bit like men, while men were encouraged to behave a little bit like women. This was called androgyny, which referred to a combination of gender-typical and gender-atypical characteristics within individuals.[1]

This androgynous trend pervades the fashion world today. It is stamped on men and women's attire, folded into their hairstyles and distilled into their perfumes, profoundly influencing society.[2] Austrian fashion designer Helmut Lang, for example, explains why he incorporates an androgynous look into his designs:

---

1. Margaret Schneider, review of *Sissies and Tomboys: Gender Nonconformity and Homosexual Childhood*, ed. Matthew Rottnekin, *The Journal of Sex Research*, Vol. 37, no. 3, p. 298.
2. For an insight on how the world of fashion profoundly influences individuals, families and peoples, see Plinio Corrêa de Oliveira, *Revolution and Counter-Revolution*, p. 63.

"We know that women are at the same time feminine and masculine, and that men are also feminine and masculine. It all depends on the degree unto which each one has assumed it, but that's the way it is."[3]

ANDROGYNY AND THE HOMOSEXUAL IDEOLOGY

This desire to mix male and female into a new androgynous gender lies at the core of the homosexual ideology. Indeed, the movement's founder Harry Hay starts off his manifesto founding the Mattachine Society with the words, "We, the androgynes of the world…"[4]

Homosexual writer Paul Varnell relates how Hay gave vital importance to androgyny:

> Hay's "idealism" had three components: a) gays are qualitatively different from heterosexuals, mentally, psychologically, spiritually, not just in "what they do in bed;" b) the core difference lies in the natural androgyny of homosexuals, that they embody both male and female elements; and c) in order to help promote their acceptance gays need to explain the contribution this difference makes to society.[5]

Michel Foucault, another homosexual theorist, writes:

> Homosexuality appeared as one of the forms of sexuality when it was transposed from the practice of sodomy onto a kind of superior androgyny, a hermaphroditism of the soul. The sodomite had been a temporary

3. Paco Alcaide, "The Man of the New Millenium," www.fashionclick.com/FC26/FC26_fashion_Men03.htm.
4. "Harry Hay," www.sciencedaily.com/encyclopedia/Harry_Hay.
5. Varnell, "Harry Hay: One Big Idea."

aberration; the homosexual was now a species.[6]

In his study "Androgyny: The Pagan Sexual Ideal," Dr. Peter Jones of the Westminster Theological Seminary in Escondido, California, links pagan androgyny to the homosexual movement.

Dr. Jones shows that it was very common in pagan religions of antiquity and among indigenous peoples in the New World, Africa and Australia for the priest figure (medicine man/shaman) to be androgynous, an effeminate man in female dress. This obsession with an androgynous being with special mystical powers continued during the Christian and Modern eras, as seen in the medieval alchemists, the theosophy of Madam Blavatsky and the sexual magic of Aleister Crowley.[7]

Dr. Jones quotes homosexual scholars who discuss this religious or mystical dimension of homosexuality. For example, Emily Culpepper, a lesbian and an associate professor of religion at the University of Redlands in Southern California, claims that homosexuals and lesbians are "shamans for a future age."[8] Another lesbian, author Virginia Mollenkott, declares: "We are God's Ambassadors."[9] J. Michael Clark, a homosexual professor at Emory University, says: "Something in our gay/lesbian being as an all-encompassing existential standpoint... appears to heighten our spiritual capacities."

Dr. Jones comments on Prof. Clark's androgynous spiritual insight:

---

6. Michel Foucault, *The History of Sexuality: Volume 1 and Introduction* (New York: Vintage, 1980), p. 43. Hermaphrodite is a plant or animal having both male and female reproductive organs.

7. Peter Jones, "Androgyny: The Pagan Sexual Ideal," *Journal of the Evangelical Theological Society*, Sept. 2000, pp. 453-454.

8. Emily Culpepper, "The Spiritual, Political Journey of a Feminist Freethinker," in *After Patriarchy: Feminist Transformations of the World Religions* (Maryknoll, N.Y.: Orbis, 1991), p. 164, quoted in Jones, p. 456.

9. Virginia Mollenkott, *Sensuous Spirituality: Out From Fundamentalism* (New York: Crossroads, 1992), p. 166.

Clark turns to Native American animism for an acceptable spiritual model.... Specifically, for Clark, the berdache, an androgynous American Indian shaman, born as a male, but as an adult choosing to live as a female, constitutes a desirable gay spiritual model, for the berdache achieves "the reunion of the cosmic, sexual and moral polarities."[10]

Harry Hay undoubtedly saw the androgynous berdache as a mediator to reunite "the cosmic, sexual and moral polarities." In fact, Hay's interest in androgynous berdaches and how they could contribute to homosexual ideology was so vivid that he moved to New Mexico to research their past.[11]

RADICAL FAERIES—BREAKING WITH CHRISTIANITY

In 1979, having moved to Hollywood, Hay founded the Radical Faeries. This movement embraced Hay's recently elaborated philosophical worldview of a society based on homosexual "subject-subject consciousness."[12]

Hay dreamed of a new society founded on this androgynous superiority of homosexuals.[13] Moreover, it represents a complete rupture with Christianity and the social order based on natural law. In his obituary of Harry Hay, Michael Bronski explains:

The spiritual core of the Radical Faeries was the

---

10. Jones, p. 464.
11. Cf. Timmons, *The Trouble with Harry Hay*, pp. 194-197, 200, 233, 235-236, 286; Harry Hay, "Radical Faerie Proposals to the 'March on Washington' Organizing Meeting," Will Roscoe, ed., *Radically Gay: Gay Liberation in the Words of Its Founder* (Boston: Beacon Press, 1996), p. 272.
12. As shown later in this chapter, Hay's "subject-SUBJECT consciousness" is a radical denial of Aristotelian philosophy and the Christian social and moral orders. Hay saw today's world—the remnants of Christian civilization—as "binary" or "subject-OBJECT" based.
13. Cf. "Excerpt from Harry Hay's Keynote for the First Annual Celebrating Gay Spirit Visions Conference," www.geocities.com/WestHollywood/Heights/5347/gsv.html.

same as the one Hay had envisioned for his original Mattachine Society: the conviction that **gay men were spiritually different from other people**. They were more in touch with nature, bodily pleasure, and **the true essence of human nature, which embraced both male and female**. Hay's spiritual radicalism had its roots in 17th century British dissenting religious groups such as the Diggers, Ranters, Quakers, and Levelers, who sought to refashion the world after their egalitarian, socialist, non-hierarchical, utopian views. Unlike his dissenting predecessors, however, it wasn't millennial Christianity that drove Hay, but a belief that sexuality was sacred.[14]

HOMOSEXUAL NEOPAGAN RITUALS

The first Radical Faerie gathering—described as a Spiritual Conference for Radical Faeries—was held over Labor Day weekend, 1979, in Benson, Arizona. "The conference was issued as a 'call' in the Sufi sense."[15] Over 200 homosexuals attended this spiritual experience imbued with pagan overtones.[16] "At the first Radical Faerie circle that evening, a spontaneous theme of paganism emerged. Invocations were offered to spirits; blessings and chants rose and fell."[17]

On one of the days, some forty naked homosexuals engaged in a mud ritual that might be called an anti-baptism. Mixing water with the clay soil, they covered themselves with red mud.[18] There

---

14. Michael Bronski, "The Real Harry Hay," *The Boston Phoenix*, Oct. 31-Nov. 7, 2002. (Our emphasis.)
15. *RFD*, no. 22 (Winter Solstice, 1979), p. 59, quoted in Margot Adler, *Drawing Down the Moon: Witches, Druids, Goddess-Worshippers, and Other Pagans in America Today* (Boston: Beacon Press, 1986), p. 341.
16. Cf. Mark Thompson, "Remembering Harry," *The Advocate*, Jan. 21, 2003, www.findarticles.com/cf_dls/m1589/2003_Jan_21/96072134/print.jhtml.
17. Timmons, *The Trouble with Harry Hay*, p. 265.
18. Cf. ibid.

was something in the ritual that evoked a primeval, tribal past, buried long ago by civilization, and, above all, by Christianity. Having molded a huge mud phallus, they crowned a mud-covered man[19] with laurel leaves and lifted him

> above everyone's heads as an "om" rumbled out of the huddled, mudded circle. A harmony and ecstasy built and seemed to go on and on. Near the ashram, as they hosed each other off in a prolonged sensual baptism, many murmured, "Scraping off the ugly green frogskins." There was an uncanny feeling of power in the mud ritual.... "Why was that little event so powerful?" I remember looking around and saying... "We're in another world. We're back in time."[20]

Timmons describes another ritual of the naked Radical Faeries at the same first gathering:

> A slowly building procession crescendoed to a cacophony. In the thick of the cathartic howling and drum beating, some people reported that a black bull wandered calmly into the midst of the group and stood with the evening star just over its shoulder. Some saw this as a visitation, a vision straight from some ancient frieze. Others doubted that such an animal could have been in the area at all. Bull or not, everyone reported having undergone a transcendent high, and,

---

19. Drawing from the contemporary accounts published in *RFD* magazine, Margot Adler suggests that the man being "initiated" was not an original conference participant but a curious bystander: "A bystander, taken by the spirit of the gathering, took off his clothes and started down the bank. Immediately there was a sense of initiation. They held him on their shoulders—a completely white body amid the mud people. They lowered him into the ooze and covered him over. They held him up high again and began to chant." Adler, p. 342.

20. Timmons, *The Trouble with Harry Hay*, p. 267.

Vices Turned Into Gods

When people forsake Revelation and natural law, their thirst for the sacred stops seeking God and pursues fantasies created by their own unrestrained imaginations. They create and adore their own gods, usually a mythical projection of their own bad habits. By thus attributing a religious dimension to their vices, they "justify" them.

The Fathers of the Church teach that the Greco-Roman pagan world turned its vices into gods. Thus, Saint Cyprian of Carthage exclaims:

> That Jupiter of theirs is not more supreme in
> dominion than in vice, inflamed with earthly love in
> the midst of his own thunders...now breaking forth
> by the help of birds to violate the purity of boys. And
> now put the question: Can he who looks upon such
> things be healthy-minded or modest? Men imitate the
> gods whom they adore, and to such miserable beings
> their crimes become their religion (*Letters* 1:8).

Indeed, men do make a religion of their vices, and absurd doctrines are reflected in absurd cults. In Ancient Greece, for example, a large symbolic representation of a phallus was carried on a float in the processions to worship Dionysus, the god of wine and of an orgiastic religion celebrating the power and fertility of nature. Pagan Rome had its bacchanalia, drunken orgies in worship of Bacchus. The worship of Aphrodite in Greece and Astartis (or Ishtar) in Mesopotamia involved ritual prostitution. Under Canaanite influence, this same abominable practice was introduced in Israel. During these periods of infidelity of the Chosen People, even the Holy Temple of Jerusalem had rooms where the *hierodules* (ritual male and female prostitutes) carried out their rites.[21]

---

21. 1 Kings 15:12; 1 Kings 22:47; 2 Kings 23:7.

as the culmination of an extraordinary sequence, many found themselves seriously moved.[22]

MAN'S SEARCH FOR THE SPIRITUAL

No matter how hard atheists and agnostics try to deny it, human nature craves for its true end, which is God. Only the divine, the infinite and the eternal fully satisfy man's spiritual soul.

Marshall Kirk and Hunter Madsen take note of this in their book *After the Ball*. In discussing the 1979 Spiritual Conference for Radical Faeries they conclude that what homo-sexuals want "without knowing it is a return to a sense of the sacred."[23] Obviously, this is not the sacredness that comes from God. Rather, it is the false sacredness of neopaganism.

CREATING A HOMOSEXUAL NEOPAGAN WORLD

Writing in July 1980, ten months after this first Radical Faerie gathering, Harry Hay explains that he felt free to invent new rituals of fairy transformation since the old ones had been lost over centuries of Judeo-Christian "oppression."

Hay's writings provide a window into the society informed by his worldview. It would not be secular, but religious, and as all religious societies, it would have its priesthood—a homo-sexual one. Homosexuals would be the "mediators," the "berdache/shamans," "God's ambassadors." In Christian terminology, they would be the "pontiffs" (from the Latin, *pontifex* – the bridge-maker).

Just as Christianity profoundly influenced every aspect of civilization in the Christian West, so also in the society envisioned by Hay *every* aspect of life, language and culture would be infused by an anarchic, neopagan, homosexual

---

22. Ibid., p. 268. Margot Adler also describes this "large, structured ritual—the Great Faery Circle. It began with a torchlight procession..." She provides other details but does not mention a "visitation." Cf. Adler, pp. 342-343.
23. Kirk and Madsen, p. 294.

consciousness. However, Hay's world is diametrically opposed to Christianity.

This cannot happen without a radical transformation of society as we know it. In other words, using the expression of Kirk and Madsen, society must undergo "Conversion."

Hay claims that his homosexual "subject-SUBJECT consciousness" is not new. He affirms that it was known by Islam's Sufi sect, and is now "newly revealed," after being long forgotten. Hay's worldview is not new. It is only a new manifestation of ancient pagan Gnosticism.[24]

GNOSIS AND THE ANDROGYNOUS MYTH

Through the millennia, Gnosis, or Gnosticism, has been the largest wellspring of mystical eroticism. One Gnostic, occultist myth that appears in ancient and current pagan religions claims that in the beginning of Creation there existed a being that was both male and female. The Gnostic occult sects that attempted to subvert Judaism and Christianity, for example, distorted Genesis when it says, "male and female he created them," claiming that in the beginning humans were androgynous.[25] They claim a catastrophe caused the separation of the sexes into masculine and feminine, Adam and Eve.[26] Gnostic mythology claims that man's "redemption" consists in reuniting the two sexes and restoring the primeval androgynous being.[27]

---

24. Cf. "The Spiritual Roots of Homosexuality," www.spirit-alembic.com/ishvara.html.

25. Genesis says that God created man to His image and likeness and later adds that He created the two sexes, male and female. This is made clear in the subsequent chapter, which contains a more explicit history of the creation of the first man and narrates the creation of the first woman (Gen. 2:7, 18-20).

26. Harry Hay gives his homosexual version of Genesis in his 1976 essay "Christianity's First Closet Case: A Study in the Application of Gay Consciousness." Cf. Roscoe, ed., *Radically Gay*, pp. 218-233.

27. Cf. Holly Boswell, *The Spirit of Transgender*, www.homestead.com/transpir-its/files/SpiritOfTG.html; Moses Gaster, s.v. "Androgynos (Hermaphrodite)," *Jewish Encyclopedia*, www.jewishencyclopedia.com/view.jsp?artid=1508&letter=A.

A DISGUISED BUT REAL RELIGIOUS WAR

The antagonism between the homosexual movement and Christianity is much more profound than the psychological, scientific, social and political arguments so often debated. Harry Hay, the movement's founder, is clear that the antagonism is religious. Therefore, it would appear that the movement's "moral revolution" is part of an immense effort to supplant Christianity with a Gnostic, neopagan, erotic mysticism.

More than in a Cultural War, it seems America is immersed in an authentic and poorly disguised religious war.

A New Gnostic World

In promoting androgyny, the homosexual movement's great difficulty lies in explaining the existence of obvious anatomic and physiological differences between the sexes.

Activists can use means such as fashion and behavior to blur the distinctions. They can even carry out operations to adapt the body and give it characteristics of the other sex. All these accidental modifications, however, do not alter the inner nature of each sex: a man is still a man, a woman is still a woman, regardless of the mutilations or additions made to their bodies.

Thus, the movement must give an explanation that transcends the sexes, making sexual differentiation irrelevant. This presents the innermost core of the homosexual ideology: What is *reality* for them?

According to common sense and traditional philosophy, there is a clear difference between the person who knows (the subject) and the external thing known (the object).

The universe has intellectual beings that can know things and a multitude of individual beings with fixed natures, capable of being known.

In fact, the universe consists of innumerable individual beings that fall into four categories:

1) the perfect spirit, which is God;

2) pure spirits, either angels or demons;

3) human beings, which are composite beings– both spirit and matter, and

4) irrational and material beings, namely, the animals, plants and minerals.

The movement can only destroy the importance of the sexual differentiation between man and woman by destroying the differentiation between all beings. To do this, it must despise the material world as unreal or at best a transitory reality. The material world would be a sort of excrescence artificially united to a spiritual being. This is the teaching of Gnosticism.

In this Gnostic vision of the universe, all differentiation between individuals – including the distinction of genders among men – is totally unimportant.

Consequently, Gnostics consider the traditional differentiation between subject and object (in knowing) to be absurd. They make no distinction between the two, transforming all being into one, collective spiritual being.

Thus, it appears that when the homosexual movement speaks of androgyny, it refers more to a *spiritual* than a *physical* one. It uses androgyny as a metaphor to suggest a mystical state that *transcends* reality.

For Gnostics, it matters little if sexual intercourse occurs between people of the same or opposite sex. But since they believe that matter imprisons this spiritual being, they are against any sexual act favoring procreation. For Gnostics, the only *good* sexual intercourse is the homosexual one.

Although somewhat philosophical, these considerations are necessary to grasp the radical transformation of society

Harry Hay envisioned. His 1980 essay states:

> The world we inherit, the total Hetero-Male-ori-
> ented-and-dominated world of Tradition …our his-
> tory, our philosophy, our psychology, our culture,
> and very languages of communication—*all* are
> totally subject-OBJECT in concept…. Men and
> Women are—sexually, emotionally, and spiritually—
> *objects* to one another…
>
> To all of this we fairies should be, essentially,
> alien. Because those *others* with whom we seek to
> link, to engage, to slip into, to merge with are oth-
> ers *like me*, are SUBJECTS…like ME…
>
> We haven't as yet learned how to communicate
> subject-SUBJECT realities. Subject-SUBJECT is a
> multidimensional consciousness which may never
> be readily conveyable in the Hetero-male-evolved,
> two-dimensional or Binary, language to which we
> are confined….
>
> *We must re-examine every system of thought*
> *heretofore developed*, every Hetero-male-evolved
> subject-OBJECT philosophy, science, religion,
> mythology, political system, language—divesting
> them every one of their binary subject-OBJECT
> base and re-inserting subject-SUBJECT relation.
> Confronted with the loving-sharing Consensus of
> subject-SUBJECT relationships, *all Authoritar-*
> *ianism must vanish*…
>
> Fairies must begin to throw off the filthy green
> frog-skin of Hetero-imitation and discover the lovely
> Gay-Conscious not-MAN shining underneath.[28]

---

28. Harry Hay, "Toward the New Frontiers of Fairy Vision…subject-SUBJECT
    Consciousness," in Roscoe, ed., *Radically Gay*, pp. 258-263. (Emphasis and
    uppercasing in the original.)

PART II
Answering the Homosexual Movement's Arguments

CHAPTER 9
The True Purpose of the Sexual Act

The notion of sin in general, and the sin against chastity in particular, has faded to such an extent that it is fitting to recall the principles of natural law and Catholic teaching on this delicate subject.[1]

THE PURPOSE OF THE SEXUAL ACT

If sexual intercourse were not enjoyable in itself, the propagation of the human race, which depends on it, would be jeopardized. Reason makes it clear, however, that the purpose of this act is not pleasure but the perpetuation of mankind. To make pleasure the primary motive for sexual intercourse replaces the principal end of the act with its corollary. This inversion runs contrary to the act's very purpose.

Begetting new life brings with it the obligation to raise a child and care for his material needs, especially his education and character formation. This is no small responsibility and requires sacrifice and dedication.

Given man's rational nature, the bonds that unite the parents who beget new life with their children who are the fruits of their union are not ephemeral, as is the case with animals. Among animals, as soon as the offspring is full-grown, the maternal and paternal relationships usually cease to the point that parents and offspring no longer recognize each other.

Among men, on the contrary, a permanent bond of affection, responsibility and respect continues to exist between parents and their adult children. It is an affection that lasts a lifetime and even longer—not even death erases fond memories from the hearts of the living.

---

1. This chapter's brief overview is based on the arguments presented by St. Thomas Aquinas in the *Summa Theologica*, II-II, q. 153-154 and Supplement qq. 41 et. seq.; *Catechism of the Catholic Church*, nos. 369-372, 1643-1651, 2360-2391.

All this demonstrates that only the loving, permanent union between a man and a woman who desire to have children, raise them affectionately and provide mutual help throughout the vicissitudes of life provides the ideal conditions for the begetting and education of children. Hence, the conditions for sexual intercourse to entirely fulfill the noble end set down by the Creator are only found in monogamous and indissoluble matrimony.[2]

OPPOSING THE MAIN PURPOSE OF INTERCOURSE IS A SIN

Thus, anything opposed to the main purpose of sexual intercourse (procreation and the consequent upbringing of children) is evil.[3] In religious terms, it is sinful.

This main purpose can be frustrated in two ways. Firstly, this can be done by artificially avoiding conception or by engaging in sexual acts that are sterile by nature, such as self-eroticism and homosexuality.[4] Secondly, the main purpose is violated when the fecund nature of sexual intercourse per se is respected, but the parties lack the concern and conditions to

---

2. Marital intercourse also has the purpose of increasing love between the spouses and subduing concupiscence. Due to its violence, carnal pleasure tends to dominate and subjugate the mind. However, this effect is normally absent in matrimony, as St. Alphonsus Liguori explains: "Fornication is always evil, even when, at times and *per accidens*, a fornicator may raise his children well. The reason is because...it is against natural law to subject reason to the flesh, as happens in fornication, for the sake of pleasure. But in matrimony, even if the same pleasure is present, God disposes, in His special providence, that such disorder will not occur" (D. Neyraguet, *Compendio de la Teologia Moral de S. Afonso de Ligorio* [Madrid: Viuda de Palacios e Hijos Editores, 1852], p. 236).

3. According to St. Thomas, "a sin, in human acts, is that which is against the order of reason. Now the order of reason consists in its ordering everything to its end in a fitting manner.... [A]nd just as the use of food is directed to the preservation of life in the individual, so is the use of venereal acts directed to the preservation of the whole human race" (St. Thomas Aquinas, *Summa Theologica*, II-II, q. 153, a. 2).

4. Marital relations in the cases of natural sterility resulting from pathological deficiencies in either the husband or the wife are legitimate because no hindrance is being placed against normal intercourse, which only fails to produce its natural results on account of unintended, accidental causes.

raise the child properly. Such is the case with fornication, adultery, incest, seduction and rape.

Although every directly procured act of consummated lust is a mortal sin, some are graver than others. Adultery is graver than simple fornication; incest is graver than adultery; and sins against nature are graver still. Sins against nature are not only opposed to the purpose of sexual intercourse, but in addition are "contrary to the natural order of the venereal act as becoming to the human race."[5]

THE VIOLENCE OF CARNAL DESIRE IS A CONSEQUENCE OF ORIGINAL SIN

Although Our Lord Jesus Christ redeemed mankind by shedding His Most Precious Blood, and baptism erases the stain of Original Sin on our souls, the consequences of this sin remain: the weakness of the flesh and the revolt of the disorderly passions.

In the state of innocence, Adam and Eve exercised total control over their passions: "The man and his wife were both naked, yet they felt no shame."[6]

After Original Sin, however, "the eyes of both of them were opened, and they realized that they were naked; so they sewed fig leaves together and made loincloths for themselves."[7]

The disorder of Original Sin is a great trial for man. As Saint Paul says: "But I see in my members another principle at war with the law of my mind, taking me captive to the law of sin that dwells in my members."[8] But with the grace of God these bad tendencies can be overcome, as Saint Paul proclaims: "I can do all things in him who strengthens me."[9]

---

5. St. Thomas Aquinas, *Summa Theologica*, II-II, q. 154, a. 11.
6. Gen. 2:25.
7. Gen. 3:7.
8. Rom. 7:23.
9. Phil. 4:13.

Our Lord Elevated Matrimony to the Supernatural Level

Our Lord elevated matrimony to the supernatural level, making it a sacrament. He bestowed special graces on marriage, restoring it to its original dignity in the Garden of Eden, when God united Adam and Eve in holy marriage. Christian marriage is also a symbol of Christ's union with the Church, as Saint Paul teaches:

> Husbands, love your wives, even as Christ loved the church and handed himself over for her, to sanctify her, cleansing her by the bath of water with the word, that he might present to himself the church in splendor, without spot or wrinkle or any such thing, that she might be holy and without blemish. So (also) husbands should love their wives as their own bodies. He who loves his wife loves himself. For no one hates his own flesh but rather nourishes and cherishes it, even as Christ does the church, because we are members of His body. 'For this reason a man shall leave his father and his mother and be joined to his wife, and the two shall become one flesh.' This is a great mystery, but I speak in reference to Christ and the church. In any case, each one of you should love his wife as himself, and the wife should respect her husband (Eph. 5:25-33).

Because of the weakness that Original Sin left in man, moral theologians have always recommended extreme care to avoid being overcome by carnal desires. King David is a prime example of how vigilance is important. By lowering his guard and allowing himself to be captivated by Bethsabee's beauty, he ended up sinning with her and ordering the death of her husband, Urias. In the words of the Savior, "Watch ye: and pray that you enter not into temptation. The spirit indeed is willing, but the flesh is weak."[10]

LUST DEVASTATES THE INDIVIDUAL AND SOCIAL ORDER

On the individual plane, lust destroys peace of mind, nobility of soul, heavenly desires and causes spiritual blindness. The more one satisfies lust, the more vehemently it burns, provoking nervousness, excitation and impatience and often leading to other sins and even crime. Thus, lust numbers among the seven capital vices. It feeds egotism, thoughtlessness, rashness and instability. Through lust, extremely painful and sometimes even fatal sexually transmitted diseases, such as AIDS or syphilis, are contracted and spread. It can also feed morbid tendencies.

In society, lust favors corruption, fosters prostitution and pornography, renders families unstable, encourages contraception and abortion and harms the upbringing of children.[11]

CHASTITY FREES MAN

The virtue of chastity liberates man from the tyranny of concupiscence, making him more apt in noble, spiritual activities and strengthening his will for the battles of life. Saint Thomas says:

---

10. Mark 14:38. Referring to impurity in his treatise on morals, St. Alphonsus Liguori says that through this vice "more souls plunge into Hell, and I do not hesitate to say that all reprobates are condemned because of it, or at least not without it" (Neyraguet, p. 230).

11. Cf. Fr. Cornelius Damen, C.SS.R., s.v. "Lust," Francesco Card. Roberti and Msgr. Pietro Palazzini, *Dictionary of Moral Theology* (Westminster, Md.: The Newman Press, 1962), p. 719.

When the lower powers are strongly moved towards their objects, the result is that the higher powers are hindered and disordered in their acts. Now the effect of the vice of lust is that the lower appetite, namely the concupiscible, is most vehemently intent on its object, to wit, the object of pleasure, on account of the vehemence of the pleasure. Consequently the higher powers, namely the reason and the will, are most grievously disordered by lust.[12]

---

12. St. Thomas Aquinas, *Summa Theologica*, II-II, q. 153, a. 5.

The Primary End of Marriage

Professor Mark S. Latkovic, of Detroit's Sacred Heart Seminary, writes:

> It is frequently claimed that the Second Vatican Council dislodged the traditional place of procreation as the "primary end" of marriage in favor of conjugal love as primary or at least on an equal footing with procreation, thus weakening the importance of the latter.

Prof. Latkovic disagrees that the Second Vatican Council made this change. He argues that in the Pastoral Constitution *Gaudium et Spes* the Council "taught that both the 'institution of marriage' and 'conjugal love' are ordered to the procreation and education of children (cf. GS, 48)."[13]

Fr. Carlos Miguel Buela, founder and Superior General of the Institute of the Incarnate Word, is of the same opinion. He states that the Council reiterates previous Church teaching:

> Although some fail to use this precise termi-nology [of Pius XII on the primary and secondary ends of marriage] consecrated by the Magisterium of the Church, if they wish to remain within the bounds of Catholic doctrine

---

13. In support of this position, he mentions Spanish theologian Fr. Ramon Garcia de Haro. (Mark S. Latkovic, *Vatican II on Love and Marriage*, www.aodonline.org/aodonline-sqlimages/SHMS/Faculty/LatkovicMark/OpEds/LOVEANDM.pdf.)

they are obliged to recognize the reality that it translates into, whether they like it or not.

Some seek support in the Second Vatican Council to falsify or alter the essential subordination of the ends of matrimony, placing love before procreation, i.e., making the secondary end the primary one and vice versa....

In support of its doctrine, the Second Vatican Council's Pastoral Constitution *Gaudium et Spes*—in its chapter on the *Dignity of Matrimony and the Family*—quotes Pius XI's 1930 encyclical *Casti Connubii* no less than five times! This encyclical is the fundamental charter of Christian Matrimony. And in a footnote to its paragraph 48, speaking about matrimony's "various ends," *Gaudium et Spes* cites Saint Augustine, Saint Thomas Aquinas and the encyclical *Casti Connubii*, which explicitly affirms the subordination of ends.

Therefore, if the Second Vatican Council cites previous documents of Church Magisterium it is because it is simultaneously confirming the doctrine contained therein. In any case it could not be otherwise, for then we would be facing complete absurdity and incoherence.

Nevertheless, in opposition to such clear teaching of the Church's Magisterium, many continue to sustain and teach the primacy of love over procreation.

In his study, Fr. Buela recalls the Church's traditional doctrine on the various ends of matrimony:

The essential and complementary ends of matrimony are procreation and the upbringing of children, and the manifestation of mutual love. The fact that both are **essential** does not mean there is no **subordination** between them, since it is impossible for **one** thing [matrimony] to have **various ultimate** ends. The essential primary end is the procreation and upbringing of children, and the essential secondary ends are "mutual help, fostering of reciprocal love and abating concupiscence." Pius XII clearly teaches that the secondary ends, "...though established by nature, are not on the same level as the primary, let alone superior to it; on the contrary, they are essentially subordinated to it."...

If the primary end is love, matrimony loses that which constitutes it and makes it singularly distinct from any other type of society.

If the primary end is love and not the procreation and upbringing of children, matrimony is divested from the privileged status that it enjoys as coming before and standing above all other societies—including the State—as is recognized by natural law itself.

If the primary end is love, how is matrimony different from a mere "society of friends" or philanthropic associations?

If the primary end is love, why not "wash one's hands" of such a bothersome task as the upbringing of children?[14]

---

14. Fr. Carlos Miguel Buela, *Los Fines del Matrimonio* [The Ends of Marriage] in Forum of Moral Theology, Institute of the Incarnate Word, www.iveargentina.org/Foro_SAlfonso/articulos_ajenos/fines_matrimonio.htm. (Emphasis in the original.)

Canonist Javier Hervada, of the University of Navarre, Spain, also says that the Council maintained the traditional doctrine on the ends of matrimony. He cites *Gaudium et Spes*: "Marriage and conjugal love are by their nature ordained toward the begetting and educating of children." (no. 50)

Canonist Hervada then comments:

It is evident that the conjugal act is ordered to procreation. Its natural structure is none other than the act of impregnation of a woman by a man through the use of the spouses' reproductive organs.[15]

15. Fr. Javier Hervada *Los Fines del Matrimonio*, www.encuentra.com/includes/documento.php?IdDoc=2297&IdSec=411.

CHAPTER 10
The Impossibility of True Homosexual Love

"Homosexual love" is another myth which homosexual activists use to justify their ideology and stake their claim to same-sex "marriage."

Prof. Chai Feldblum, a same-sex "marriage" and homosexual rights advocate, highlighted the importance of this myth: "Real change will come when the public recognizes gay love not just as morally neutral, but as morally good, to the same extent that straight love is good."[1]

Can one speak of "homosexual love?" Could there be a variant on par with true love? To answer this, true love must be defined. For this end, Saint Thomas Aquinas, the Angelic Doctor, provides valuable insight.[2]

A PLEASING ATTRACTION

Love is an attraction to a good perceived in something or someone with whom one feels connatural and pleased. Love has its most profound root in man's inclination to God, the Supreme Good. While attracting all creatures to Himself, God also moves them to desire partial goods insofar as they participate in the infinite good. This is why Saint John teaches that "we love, because He [God] first loved us."[3]

Human beings can feel this pleasing attraction to persons, animals, things, places, sounds, arts, activities and other objects.

In itself, love is immaterial and resides above all in the will. It resonates physically with emotions and sentiments. Love has degrees and is subject to distortion due to the effects of Original Sin on man.

---

1. Quoted in Laura Secor, "Rainbow Warriors."
2. Cf. St. Thomas Aquinas, *In Ethicorum*, lib. 8, lectio 12, nos. 18-24. (Our translation.); *Summa Theologica* I, q. 20, aa. 1,3; q. 60, aa. 1-5; I-II, q. 25, a. 2, q. 26, aa. 1,4, q. 27, aa. 1-3; *Summa Contra Gentiles*, I, C. 91.
3. 1 John 4:19.

TWO FORMS OF LOVE: DESIRE AND FRIENDSHIP

There are two forms of love. The first is a lower and imperfect form of love called *love of desire (amor concupiscentiae)* or *sensitive love*. Involving predominantly the senses, it is especially directed towards objects, things, places, animals and so on.

The second is a superior and properly human form of love which is called the *love of friendship (amor amicitiae)* or *volitional love*. It resides above all in the will and results from affinity between human beings.[4] In its highest state, this *love of friendship* requires that the person come out of himself and love another not for his own enjoyment and interest but for the other's good: "For a friend is another myself," and "The lover stands in relation to that which he loves, as though it were himself or part of himself."[5]

However, human beings are not pure spirits like the angels, or God, the Perfect Spirit. Man is a composite of body and soul, matter and spirit. Hence, however spiritual man's love may be, it still affects his sensibility, as an emotion or sentiment.

Though legitimate and important, this sensible component cannot be the essence of love. Emotion or sentiment cannot dominate the properly spiritual nature of true love, which tends to infinity.

As Saint Thomas Aquinas explains, practicing the virtue of temperance keeps the balance between the spiritual and the sensitive components. It orients the sentiments, and masters or refines the sensibility. Temperance provides man with balance, especially in those actions and sentiments more directly linked to the instincts of self-preservation and procreation.[6]

---

4. Here we are dealing only with natural love and not with supernatural love, charity.
5. St. Thomas Aquinas, *In Ethic.*, lib. 8, l. 1 n. 6; *Summa Theologica*, I-II, q. 26, a. 2, ad. 2.
6. "Desire denotes an impulse of the appetite towards the object of pleasure and this impulse needs control, which belongs to temperance" (*Summa Theologica*, II-II, q. 141, a. 3 ad 2).

DISTORTIONS OF THE LOVE OF FRIENDSHIP

Without the moderating effect of temperance, the sheer violence of desire can dominate a relationship of friendship. This dominance can transform the love of friendship into a love of desire. Accordingly, the good of the other can be replaced by self-interest where the main goal becomes securing one's own advantage.

In this case, which often happens in romantic affairs, the relationship becomes egotistical. Sometimes both parties share this egotism, which Madame de Staël rightly dubbed "egotism in tandem."

People who are the object of this passion or egotistical interest are loved neither for their own sake nor for what they are worth. Rather they are loved only insofar as they fulfill the interests or wishes of the other. This is not true love; it only has the appearance or accidental trappings of real love.[7]

REASON GUIDES GENUINE HUMAN LOVE

The more a relationship is dominated by a love of desire and thus the sensibility, the farther it is from properly human love. Since the intellect and will do not dominate the relationship, it edges closer to the mere attraction proper to animals. Reason rules authentically human love. As Saint Thomas Aquinas teaches, "our sensitive appetite surpasses that of other animals by reason of a certain excellence consisting in its natural aptitude to obey the reason."[8]

---

7. "Friendship based on usefulness or pleasure is friendship only accidentally. Obviously, such friendships are easily undone" (St. Thomas Aquinas, *In Ethic.* lib. 8, l. 3 n. 4).
8. *Summa Theologica*, I-II, q. 74, a. 3 ad 1.

CONJUGAL LOVE:
A FORM OF THE LOVE OF FRIENDSHIP

By their very anatomic, physiological and psychological makeup, the sexes mutually attract each other spiritually and physically. This gives rise to a special form of the love of friendship called *conjugal love*, with its fecund and selfless plenitude that results in the begetting, protection and raising of children. Although *conjugal love* satisfies the natural propensity of man's instincts, it is not blindly dependent on them.

As Saint Thomas says, "By its rationality, *conjugal love* is proper only to man …[It] is ordained not only for begetting but also for raising [of offspring] and providing for the home."[9]

In sum, *conjugal love* is a selfless or altruistic *love of friendship*, while also useful and pleasurable:

> [*Conjugal love*] is useful insofar as it fulfills the needs of domestic life and gives pleasure in the act of procreation; and when the spouses are virtuous their friendship transcends these legitimate aspects, existing because of virtue.[10]

This spiritual dimension of marital love, fundamentally altruistic, gives solidity to marriage; when it falters, decays or withers, marriages often break up.

THE IMPOSSIBILITY OF HOMOSEXUAL LOVE

Therefore, love in its proper sense is a benevolent, altruistic sentiment guided by reason and the will. "Homosexual love" is impossible because it seeks to transform the love of friendship between people of the same sex into conjugal love.[11]

---

9. St. Thomas Aquinas, *In Ethic.*, lib. 8, l. 12 nos. 20-21.
10. St. Thomas Aquinas, *In Ethic.*, lib. 8, l. 12 n. 22.
11. When we say that homosexuals do not truly love, we are referring only to the erotic homosexual passion and not to other types of love such as filial love, brotherly love and so forth, which have nothing to do with homosexuality.

Since conjugal love requires psychological and physical complementarity, it can only exist between opposite sexes.

"Homosexual love" is only a sentimental attraction of a sexual nature or a psychological dependency due to a lack of emotional or sentimental self-control. It is, therefore, a neurotic sentimentality.[12]

DESTRUCTION OF FRIENDSHIP AND SOCIAL LIFE

Indeed, "homosexual love" is neither *conjugal love* nor can it stay on the level of *love of friendship* without erotic connotations. Hence, homosexuality undermines the family and social life.

The family is the foundation of society, and marriage is the condition that gives rise to the family. Homosexuality undermines marriage by seeking to usurp its rights: Conjugal relationships are only possible between a man and a woman.

Likewise, friendship is the mortar of social life and the foundation of social concord. Without friendship, it is impossible to avoid social discord, which opens the gates to chaos

---

12 Dutch psychologist Gerard J.M. van den Aardweg, Ph.D., a specialist on homosexuality, writes: "The term *neurotic* describes such relationships well. It suggests the ego-centeredness of the relationship; the *attention-seeking* instead of loving.... *Neurotic*, in short, suggests all kinds of dramas and childish conflicts as well as the basic disinterestedness in the partner, notwithstanding the shallow pretensions of 'love.' Nowhere is there more self-deception in the homosexual than in his representation of himself as a lover. One partner is important to the other only insofar as he satisfies that other's needs. Real, unselfish love for a desired partner would, in fact, end up destroying homosexual 'love'!" (Gerard J.M. van den Aardweg, *The Battle for Normality* [San Francisco: Ignatius Press, 1997], pp. 62-63). Dr. van den Aardweg's consideration is confirmed by the following testimony in *The Gay Report*: "My own personal concept of being in love is being in lust.... It seems that as soon as my potential partner is totally available to me, and there is a security between us, this 'feeling' goes away, and I am no longer with the feeling. The initial feeling is replaced by resignation and eventually boredom, and then disgust, and divorce. As far as 'wanting' or 'giving' love, this is too far out for me to go into." Karla Jay and Allen Young, *The Gay Report* (New York: Summit Books, 1979), pp. 182-183.

and anarchy.[13] Since homosexuality is focused on sexual inter-course, it thereby destroys the possibility of true friendship between people of the same sex, turning friends into objects of desire or competitors in the market of passions.[14] This destroys friendship, which makes social life safe and amenable.

WEAKENING ALL SOCIETY

By weakening the family and friendship in society, the homosexual offensive destroys the foundations of society and leads it towards disintegration and anarchy.

This reality is obfuscated by the homosexual movement's use of words like "love" and "tolerance."

---

13. "Society is maintained through friendship...so let legislators do their utmost to preserve friendship among citizens...to avoid dissensions; for concord is assimilated to friendship" (St. Thomas Aquinas, *In Ethic.*, lib. 8, l. 1 n. 5).

14. "[Gay men] see one another as potential competition *and* as mere sex objects" (Kirk and Madsen, p. 323).

CHAPTER 11
Answering the Movement's Scientific Arguments

In its effort to give homosexuality all the appearances of normality, the homosexual movement has turned to science in an attempt to prove three major premises:
1) homosexuality is genetic or innate;
2) homosexuality is irreversible;
3) since animals engage in same-sex sexual behavior, it is natural.

Liberal media have been only too willing to anticipate the verdict of the scientific community and spread the false impression that science validates homosexuality. The evidence could not be more contrary.

"I WAS BORN THAT WAY!"

The argument that homosexuals are "born that way" or "it is in the genes" has led to a quest for a homosexual gene. Three research projects have been commonly misinterpreted to support that conclusion, namely those of Dr. Simon LeVay, Drs. J. Michael Bailey and Richard C. Pillard, and Dr. Dean Hamer.[1]

The Catholic Medical Association summarizes the facts in *Homosexuality and Hope*:

> A number of researchers have sought to find a biological cause for same-sexual attraction. The media have promoted the idea that a "gay gene" has already been discovered...but, in spite of several attempts,

---

1. Simon LeVay, "A Difference in Hypothalamic Structure Between Heterosexual and Homosexual Men," 253 *Science*, 1034 (1991). J. Michael Bailey and Richard C. Pillard, "A Genetic Study of Male Sexual Orientation," 48 *Archives of General Psychiatry*, 1089 (1991). Dean H. Hamer et al., "A Linkage Between DNA Markers on the X Chromosome and Male Sexual Orientation" in *The Science of Desire* (New York: Simon & Schuster, 1995), Appendix A.

none of the much-publicized studies…has been scientifically replicated. A number of authors have carefully reviewed these studies and found that not only do the studies not prove a genetic basis for same-sex attraction; the reports do not even contain such claims….

If same-sex attraction were genetically determined, then one would expect identical twins to be identical in their sexual attractions. There are, however, numerous reports of identical twins who are not identical in their sexual attractions.[2]

- **Dr. Simon LeVay's Study**

Dr. LeVay's brain research focused on a cluster of cells in the hypothalamus known as INAH-3. He claimed to have found "subtle, but significant differences" between the brain structures of homosexual and normal men. He concluded a summary of his study saying, "This finding…suggests that sexual orientation has a biological substrate."[3]

So much wild speculation followed the publication of his study in *Science Magazine* that Dr. LeVay felt compelled to set the record straight. In 1993, he wrote:

> To many people, finding a difference in brain structure between gay and straight men is equivalent to proving that gay men are "born that way." Time and again I have been described as someone who "proved that homosexuality is genetic," or some such thing. I did not. My observations were made only on adults who had been sexually active for a considerable period of time. It is not possible, purely

---

2. *Homosexuality and Hope* (Catholic Medical Association, 2000) p. 2. (Original footnotes omitted throughout.) See also Gerard J.M. van den Aardweg, p. 25.
3. Simon LeVay, *The Sexual Brain* (Cambridge, Mass.: The MIT Press, 1993), p. xii.

on the basis of my observations, to say whether the structural differences were present at birth, and later influenced the men to become gay or straight, or whether they arose in adult life, perhaps as a result of the men's sexual behavior.[4]

Dr. LeVay's insistence on more extensive observation is the crux of the whole problem. Explaining research done by a neuroscience professor at the University of California at Berkeley, Dr. A. Dean Byrd says:

> [Professor] Breedlove concluded that the brain is not a static organ. It changes and adjusts to behavior, and, in the case of his study, specifically to sexual behavior. Thus, when someone engages in a particular act repeatedly, certain neural pathways in the brain are strengthened. Since the brain is a physical organ, when these neural pathways are strengthened, it is reflected in the chemistry of the brain. Someone who repeatedly plays basketball will have a different brain than someone who studies rocket science. Likewise, a homosexual person's behavior likely causes a different resulting brain structure. Studies such as LeVay's, even if conclusive, show only what science already knows about the brain.[5]

- **The Bailey and Pillard Study**

The Bailey and Pillard study focused on twins. As the Catholic Medical Association study points out, if homosexuality is genetic, identical twins, who share the exact same genetic code, should have identical attitudes towards homosexuality.

---

4. Ibid., p. 122.
5. Dr. A. Dean Byrd and Stony Olsen, "Homosexuality: Innate and Immutable?" *Regent University Law Review*, Vol. 14, pp. 516-517. (Original footnotes omitted.)

However, Drs. Bailey and Pillard were unable to establish this. Their study did prove that when one identical twin was a homosexual there was an approximately 50/50 chance the other twin would also be homosexual. However, this 50/50 chance is more likely attributable to the influence of the surrounding culture and the other twin.

As Dr. Byrd points out: "The only essential point that surfaced from Bailey and Pillard's research actually proved that environmental influences play a strong role in the development of homosexuality."[6]

- **Dr. Dean H. Hamer's study**

Many people mistakenly believe that Dr. Dean H. Hamer discovered the "gay gene." His DNA research focused on a small stretch of the X chromosome at position Xq28. After analyzing this DNA sequence in forty pairs of homosexual brothers, he concluded that the same genetic markers existed in 83% of them.

His findings were misinterpreted to prove that homosexuality is genetic and hereditary. However, as Dr. Hamer himself affirmed:

> The pedigree failed to produce what we originally hoped to find: simple Mendelian inheritance. In fact, we never found a single family in which homosexuality was distributed in the obvious pattern that Mendel observed in his pea plants.[7]

Dr. George Rice replicated Dr. Hamer's research, but with different results. This led Dr. Rice to conclude, "Our data do not support the presence of a gene of large effect influencing

6. Ibid., p. 523.
7. Hamer and Copeland, p. 104.

sexual orientation at position Xq28."[8]

Neil Whitehead, a Ph.D. in biochemistry, affirmed: "Homosexuality is not inborn, not genetically dictated, not immutable."[9]

"I CAN'T CHANGE!"

Nothing is more devastating to the homosexual agenda than the claim that homosexuality can be cured. Indeed, if homosexuality is genetic, dominant and irreversible, then no one is responsible for deviant sexual acts since it cannot be resisted or changed even if desired.

The incontestable fact, however, is that moving past homosexual behavior, psychological therapy has proven successful in diminishing, and in many cases even eliminating, *undesired* same-sex attraction. This makes radical homosexual activists cringe.[10]

For this reason, the homosexual movement displays a marked aversion toward those who would suggest that homosexuality can be reversed or cured. For example, Dr. C. C. Tripp stated in a public debate: "There is not a single recorded instance of a change in homosexual orientation which has been validated by outside judges or testing."[11]

Based on his professional experience, Dr. Lawrence Hatterer answered:

---

8. George Rice, et al., "Male Homosexuality: Absence of Linkage to Microsatellite Markers at Xq28," *Science*, Vol. 284, p. 667.
9. Neil and Briar Whitehead, *My Genes Made Me Do It! A Scientific Look at Sexual Orientation* (Lafayette, La.: Huntington House Publishers, 1999), p. 9.
10. Personal testimonies from ex-homosexuals can be found at www.narth.com/ menus/interviews.html and http://couragerc.net/MemberTestimonies.html.
    For examples of pro-homosexual animosity for successful therapy, see Dr. Gregory Herek at www.psychology.ucdavis.edu/rainbow/html/facts_changing.html, DignityUSA at www.dignityusa.org/news/981008exgay.html, GLAAD at www.glaad.org/media/archive_detail.php?id=133.
11. *Homosexuality and Hope*, p. 6.

> I have "cured" many homosexuals…. Any other
> researcher may examine my work because it is all
> documented on 10 years of tape recordings. Many of
> these "cured" (I prefer to use the word "changed")
> patients have married, had families and live happy
> lives. It is a destructive myth that "once a homosexual,
> always a homosexual."[12]

Faced with the evidence, even Dr. Robert L. Spitzer, who
led the campaign inside the American Psychiatric Association
to discontinue listing homosexuality as a psychiatric disorder,
changed his view: "Like most psychiatrists, I thought that homosexual behavior could be resisted, but sexual orientation could not
be changed. I now believe that's untrue—some people can and do
change."[13]

In a 2001 study of 200 ex-homosexuals, Dr. Spitzer found
that religion was a very important reason many had abandoned
homosexuality: "The two most common reasons for seeking
change were that living as a gay man or lesbian was no longer
satisfying (81%) and that same-sex behavior was at odds with the
participant's religion (79%)."[14]

Therapy's significant positive results simply cannot be
ignored. The Catholic Medical Association's *Homosexuality
and Hope* statement observes:

> A number of therapists have written extensively on
> the positive results of therapy for same-sex
> attraction…. Reviews of treatment for unwanted

---

12. Ibid.
13. "Prominent Psychiatrist Announces New Study Results: 'Some Gays Can
    Change,'" www.narth.com/docs/spitzer2.html.
14. Warren Throckmorton, "Initial Empirical and Clinical Findings Concerning the
    Change Process of Ex-Gays," *Professional Psychology: Research and Practice*,
    2002, Vol. 3, p. 246.

same-sex attractions show that it is as successful as treatment for similar psychological problems: About 30% experience a freedom from symptoms and another 30% experience improvement.

Reports from individual therapists have been equally positive.... This is only a representative sampling of the therapists who report successful results in the treatment of persons experiencing same-sex attraction.[15]

If therapy for unwanted same-sex attraction registers a 30% success rate (and another 30% are partially cured) in today's hedonistic society, how much more success could be expected in a truly Catholic culture which provides all the elements for the practice of virtue?

"IF ANIMALS DO IT, THEN IT MUST BE NATURAL"

Aware of the scientific weakness of their first two premises, homosexual activists often use the third premise based on animal behavior.

The reasoning behind this third homosexual scientific premise could be stated as follows: "Homosexual behavior is observable in animals. Animals follow their instincts in accordance with their nature. Therefore, homosexuality is in accordance with animal nature. Since man is also animal, then homosexuality must also be in accordance with human nature."

• Are filicide and cannibalism also part of human nature?

This homosexual line of reasoning is unsustainable. Those who apply it to seemingly homosexual acts among animals must also accept that other forms of animal behavior such as parental killing of offspring, or intra-species devouring,

---

15. *Homosexuality and Hope*, p. 7.

are also in accordance with animal nature.[16]

Applying this reasoning to man (because he is also an animal) would force the acceptance of the absurd conclusion that filicide and cannibalism are according to human nature.[17]

- **A "homosexual instinct" does not exist in animals**

Anyone engaged in the most elementary animal observation is forced to conclude that animal "homosexuality," filicide and cannibalism are exceptions to normal animal behavior. Consequently, one cannot speak of them as instincts in animal nature. These observable and exceptional forms of animal behavior result from other factors beyond the normal instincts.

- **Explaining the problem: clashing stimuli and confused instincts**

In explaining the problem of these behaviors, the first observation must be the fact that animal instincts are not bound by the absolute determinism of the physical laws governing the mineral world. In varying degrees, all living beings can adapt somewhat to circumstances. They respond to internal or external stimuli.

Secondly, animal cognition is purely sensorial, limited to sounds, odors, touch, tastes and images. Thus, they do not have the precision and clarity of human intellectual perception.

---

16. Cf. Sarah Hartwell, "Cats that kill kittens," www.messybeast.com/ kill_kit.htm. Also, "Cannibalism in Animals," www.hamshahri.org/musiems/daarabad/ inwm/no.8/english/wnw/wnw01.html.

17. "It is a frequent error for people to contrast human and animal behaviors, as if the two were homogenous. We see, for example, acts of unspeakable ferocity among animals, such as the killing of offspring, the weaker individuals, and the partner after mating. This does not mean that men should adjust their lives to the pattern followed by irrational beings not gifted with individual conscience. The laws ruling human behavior are of a different nature and they should be sought where God inscribed them, namely, in human nature" (Bruto Maria Bruti, *Domande e risposte sul problema dell'omosessualità*, at www.paginecattoliche.it/domande_omosessualita.htm).

Therefore, it is not infrequent that animals confuse one sensation for another or one object with another.

Instincts move an animal toward a purpose in accordance with its nature. However, the spontaneous thrust of the instinctive impulse can suffer modifications as it runs its course, since other sensorial images, perceptions or memories can come into play as new stimuli affecting the animal's behavior. Also, the conflict of two or more instincts can sometimes modify the original impulse.

In man, when two instinctive reactions clash, the intellect determines the best course to follow, and the will then holds one instinct in check while encouraging the other.

With animals, given the absence of intellect and will, when two instinctive impulses clash, the one most favored by circumstances prevails. This results in observable cases of animal filicide, cannibalism and "homosexuality."

- **Animal filicide**

Sarah Hartwell explains that tomcats kill their kittens as a result of receiving mixed signals from their instincts:

> Most female cats can switch between "play mode" and "hunt mode" in order not to harm their offspring. In tomcats this switching off of "hunt mode" may be incomplete and, when they become highly aroused through play, the "hunting" instinct comes into force and they may kill the kittens. The hunting instinct is so strong, and so hard to switch off when prey is present, that dismemberment and even eating of the kitten may ensue.... **Compare the size, sound and activity of kittens with the size, sound and activity of prey. They are both small, have high-pitched voices and move with fast, erratic movements. All of these**

trigger hunting behavior. In the tomcat, maternal behavior cannot always override hunting behavior and he treats the kittens in exactly the same way he would treat small prey. **His instincts are confused.**[18]

- **Animal cannibalism**

Regarding animal cannibalism, the magazine *Iran Nature and Wildlife Magazine* comments:

> [A] cannibal is an animal which feeds on others of its own species…. Around 140 different species show cannibalistic tendencies under various conditions. Cannibalism is most common among lower verte-brates and invertebrates, often due to a predatory animal **mistaking one of its own kind for prey**. But it also occurs among birds and mammals, especially when food is scarce.[19]

- **Animal "homosexual" behavior**

Exactly because animals lack reason, their means of expressing their affective states (fear, pleasure, pain, desire, etc.) are limited. Animals lack the rich resources at man's disposal to adapt their way of talking, gazing and gesturing to express sentiments. Consequently, animals often express their affective states ambiguously. They borrow, so to speak, the manifestations of the instinct of reproduction to manifest the instincts of dominance, aggressiveness, fear, gregariousness and so on.

A typical example of this phenomenon can be seen with bonobos. These mammals from the chimpanzee family engage in seemingly sexual behavior. These sexual attitudes are their

---

18. Sarah Hartwell, "Cats that kill kittens." (Our emphasis.)
19. "Cannibalism in Animals." (Our emphasis.)

way of expressing dominance, fear, acceptance and other affective states. Thus, Frans B. M. de Waal, who spent hundreds of hours observing and filming bonobos, says:

> There are two reasons to believe sexual activity [behavior] is the bonobo's answer to **avoiding conflict**. First, anything, not just food, that arouses the interest of more than one bonobo at a time tends to result in sexual contact. If two bonobos approach a cardboard box thrown into their enclosure, they will briefly mount each other before playing with the box. Such situations lead to squabbles in most other species. But bonobos are quite tolerant, perhaps because they use sex to divert attention and to **diffuse tension**.
>
> Second, **bonobo sex often occurs in aggressive contexts** totally unrelated to food. A jealous male might chase another away from a female, after which the two males reunite and engage in scrotal rubbing. Or after a female hits a juvenile, the latter's mother may **lunge at the aggressor**, an action that is immediately followed by genital rubbing between the two adults.[20]

Another explanation for apparent "homosexual" behavior among animals is confusion in identifying the other sex properly. The lower the species in the animal scale, the more tenuous and difficult to detect are the differences between sexes, leading to more frequent confusion.

In any case, the fact remains that whatever "homosexual" appearances animal behavior may assume, they do not stem

---

20. Frans B. M. de Waal, "Bonobo Sex and Society," *Scientific American*, Mar. 1995, pp. 82-88, www.songweaver.com/info/bonobos.html. (Our emphasis.)

from a "homosexual" instinct that is part of animal nature. Dr. Antonio Pardo, Professor of Bioethics at the University of Navarre, Spain, explains:

> Properly speaking, homosexuality does not exist among animals.... For reasons of survival, the reproductive instinct among animals is always directed towards an individual of the opposite sex. Therefore, an animal can never be homosexual as such. Nevertheless, the interaction of other instincts (particularly dominance) can result in behavior that appears to be homosexual. Such behavior cannot be equated with an animal homosexuality. All it means is that animal sexual behavior encompasses aspects beyond that of reproduction.[21]

In conclusion, homosexuality is not only contrary to man's rational nature, but even animal nature.

21. Antonio Pardo, "Aspectos médicos de la homosexualidad," *Nuestro Tiempo*, Jul.-Aug. 1995, pp. 82-89.

CHAPTER 12
Answering Twelve Arguments Used
to Push the Homosexual Agenda

Besides appealing to science, homosexual activists also further their agenda with other arguments. Some stem from liberal interpretations of fundamental human or constitutional rights. Others flow from liberal philosophical or religious beliefs.

All these arguments seek to justify same-sex "marriage," whether under this name or the euphemistically labeled "civil unions" or "domestic partnerships." The acceptance of any of these contentions will redefine the concept of marriage in total disregard for its true nature. If this happens, law loses its foundation in the natural order and right reason and thus its legitimacy.[1]

These arguments employed by the homosexual movement will be examined here from the perspective of natural law. Arguments from "Catholic" homosexual activists[2] are examined in light of Church doctrine.

"WE'RE EQUAL IN THE EYES OF
THE LAW, SO WE'RE GETTING MARRIED!"

It is true that everyone is equal in the eyes of the law. This equality, however, is juridical, not biological. It does not and indeed cannot eliminate the anatomical and psychological differences between the sexes. It is these very differences that

---

1. "As Augustine says (De Lib. Arb. i, 5) 'that which is not just seems to be no law at all': wherefore the force of a law depends on the extent of its justice. Now in human affairs a thing is said to be just, from being right, according to the rule of reason. But the first rule of reason is the law of nature, as is clear from what has been stated above (Q. 91, Art. 2 ad 2). Consequently every human law has just so much of the nature of law, as it is derived from the law of nature. But if in any point it deflects from the law of nature, it is no longer a law but a perversion of law" (St. Thomas Aquinas, *Summa Theologica*, II-I, q. 95, a. 2).
2. Cf. Andrew Sullivan, "Gay Marriage," www.slate.msn.com/id/3642/entry/23844/, "Why 'Civil Union' Isn't Marriage," www.indegayforum.org/authors/sullivan/sullivan4.html, "Who Says the Church Can't Change?" *Time*, June 17, 2002.

create the conditions for marriage and constitute its natural foundation.

Regarding marriage, juridical equality means that all those with the natural *capacity* to marry have the *right* to do so. This juridical equality does not *create* the conditions required by nature for marriage. Now the conjugal act is intrinsically related to marriage, and nature requires two individuals from opposite sexes for its performance.

This natural requirement is totally lacking in two people of the same sex who wish to marry, so the principle of equality under the law does not apply.

"WE CAN DO WHATEVER WE WANT AS LONG AS WE DON'T INFRINGE ON OTHER PEOPLE'S RIGHTS!"

This concept is false. Human liberty grants man the *possibility* to act as he wishes, but not necessarily the *right* to do so. Man's actions must conform to right reason and natural law. "Nothing more foolish can be uttered or conceived than the notion that, because man is free by nature, he is therefore exempt from law."[3]

"HOMOSEXUAL ACTS BETWEEN CONSENTING ADULTS HURT NO ONE!"

Consent does not necessarily legitimize an act. The morality of an act does not depend only on the intent and consent of those who perform it; the act must also conform to moral law. Thus, the mutual consent of homosexual partners can never legitimize homosexual acts, which are unnatural deviations of the sexual act from its true and natural purpose.[4] And consensual homosexual acts do hurt. The spread of

---

3. Leo XIII, Encyclical *Libertas*, in Claudia Carlen, I.H.M., *The Papal Encyclicals 1878-1903* (New York: McGrath Publishing Co., 1981), no. 7, p. 171.
4. See Chapter 9.

homosexuality undermines public morality and the family. It "hurts" the common good of society and the perpetuation of the human race.

"WHAT WE DO IN THE PRIVACY OF OUR HOME IS NOBODY'S BUSINESS!"

The privacy of the home is undoubtedly sacred, but it is not absolute.

When an evil act is done in public, the ensuing scandal compounds its intrinsic evil. However, an evil act does not become good just because it is performed in private. Its evil nature remains unchanged.

Though homosexual acts are graver when they are public, they continue to be "intrinsically evil" when done in private.[5] Likewise, the inviolability of the home does not protect immoral and socially destructive acts such as child prostitution, polygamy, incest and any other such acts.

"MORALITY IS NONE OF THE GOVERNMENT'S BUSINESS!"

According to natural law, the State has the duty to uphold public morality. This does not mean that the State must enforce the practice of every virtue and proscribe the practice of every vice, as supposedly attempted by the ayatollahs of today. Rather, it means that, when legislating on moral matters, the government must decide when something directly affects the common good, and then legislate so as to favor virtue and obstruct vice.

---

5. "If acts are intrinsically evil, a good intention or particular circumstances can diminish their evil, but they cannot remove it. They remain 'irremediably' evil acts per se and in themselves they are not capable of being ordered to God and to the good of the person" (John Paul II, Encyclical *Veritatis Splendor*, no. 81, www.vatican.va/holy_father/john_paul_ii/encyclicals/documtnets/hf_jp-ii_enc_06081993_veritatis-splendor_en.html).

Since homosexuality, adultery, prostitution and pornography undermine the foundations of the family, the basis of society, then the State is entitled to use its coercive power to proscribe or curtail them in the interests of the common good.

"SAME-SEX 'MARRIAGE' DOES NOT THREATEN TRADITIONAL MARRIAGE. THEY CAN COEXIST SIDE BY SIDE!"

It is said that vice asks for nothing more than to sit next to virtue. When vice is allowed to peacefully coexist with virtue, the latter is corrupted. Virtue is only integral as long as it vigorously combats its opposite.

Same-sex "marriage" destroys the integrity of true marriage by turning traditional marriage into a *species* within the marriage *genus*. This broad marriage genus would supposedly encompass traditional marriage, homosexual or heterosexual unions, and whatever other bizarre new relationships might arise.[6] This new "marriage" genus, however, is not marriage.

Marriage is the permanent, sacred bond uniting a man and woman who desire to constitute a family and face life's trials together. Marriage entails selfless dedication, devotion and sacrifice. Marriage and the family are sacred institutions that foster the common good of society.

The legalization of same-sex "marriage" and its placement on equal footing with traditional marriage subverts and destroys the latter. When public authority and society in general deny true marriage's uniqueness and irreplaceable contribution to the common good, and when individuals can find its legal incentives and rewards more easily in counterfeits, then true marriage is on the road to extinction.

---

6. On June 19, 2003, media around the world trumpeted the "marriage" between a 9-year old Indian girl and a stray dog. See "Girl weds dog to break 'evil spell,'" www.news.bbc.co.uk/1/hi/world/south_asia/3004930.stm.

"SAME-SEX 'MARRIAGE' IS OPPOSED TODAY AS INTERRACIAL MARRIAGE WAS OPPOSED FIFTY YEARS AGO. IT'S PURE PREJUDICE!"

This contention is false. First of all, one cannot compare two essentially different realities. A man and a woman of different races are not comparable to two men or two women.

A man and a woman wanting to marry may be completely different in their characteristics: one may be black, the other white; one rich, the other poor; one learned, the other not; one tall, the other short; or one may be famous, the other unknown. None of these differences are insurmountable obstacles to marriage. The two individuals are still man and woman, and thus the requirements of nature are respected.

Same-sex "marriage" opposes nature. Two individuals of the same sex, regardless of their race, wealth, stature, erudition or fame, will never be able to marry because of an insurmountable biological impossibility.

There is simply no analogy between the interracial marriage of a man and a woman and the "marriage" between two individuals of the same sex.

Secondly, inherited and unchangeable racial traits cannot be compared with non-genetic and changeable behavior.

"YOU'RE SAYING WE HAVE NO RIGHTS!"

It is not true that homosexuals have no rights. Every man has the rights that flow from his rational human nature. For example, the right to life, to work and to constitute a family (not same-sex "marriage").

If two adulterers or two homosexuals exercise their right of association and go into business together, they are perfectly free to do so. The purpose of their business partnership is a legitimate one, business and trade, and the law will guarantee their rights.

It is different if they form an association to promote child pornography, pedophilia, homosexuality or adultery. Since the purpose of this association is evil, it is illegitimate, and, therefore, proscribed under natural law. No evil action per se can be the source of rights, since "the common good is the end and the rule for the State."[7]

Therefore, to forbid homosexuality or adultery does not transgress any individual fundamental natural rights since these actions are not according to human nature.

"SAME-SEX 'MARRIAGE' IS A CIVIL RIGHTS ISSUE. IT HAS NOTHING TO DO WITH MORALS!"

This is tantamount to affirming that civil rights have nothing to do with morality, which is not true. While many today disassociate the expression "civil rights" from morality, the fact is that there can be no "civil rights" without a moral foundation.

Morality is broader than and undergirds the law. Law needs to be justified in morality. Laws that are not founded on morality have no purpose, since laws exist for the good order of society. In his famous treatise on natural law, Fr. Taparelli D'Azeglio affirms:

> The moral order is the basis for society, because every duty is grounded in a moral order that results from the natural order. Now, order is the natural rule for the intellect. In the intellect, order is simply truth, and insofar as it compels the will, order is goodness.[8]

---

7. Pius XII, "Allocution of Jan. 8, 1947," the monks of Solesmes, eds., *Le Paix Interieure des Nations* (Paris: Desclée, 1952), p. 512.
8. Taparelli D'Azeglio, *Essai Théorique de Droit Naturel* (Paris: Vve. H. Casterman, 1875), Vol. I, p. 142.

"THE CHURCH ALLOWS STERILE PEOPLE TO MARRY, SO IT SHOULD BE CONSISTENT AND ALSO ALLOW SAME-SEX 'MARRIAGE!'"

This is an argument frequently used by "Catholic" homosexual activists. There is no possible comparison between the natural sterility of a married couple and the unnatural sterility of a homosexual union.

In the first case, the conjugal act performed by husband and wife has the possibility of engendering new life. Conception may not occur because of some organic dysfunction in either spouse or due to the wife's natural periods of infertility.[9] This lack of conception stems from accidental or circumstantial reasons.[10] Thus, in cases of accidental and undesired sterility in the spouses, nothing is done to frustrate the purpose of the conjugal act.

In the homosexual act, however, sterility is not accidental. It stems from the very physiology of the act, which is infertile by nature. As a Vatican 2003 document states:

> Such [homosexual] unions are not able to contribute in a proper way to the procreation and survival of the human race. The possibility of using recently discovered methods of artificial reproduction, beyond involving a grave lack of respect for human dignity, does nothing to alter this inadequacy.[11]

---

9. Sterility is distinguished from impotency. Sterility is that permanent or temporary condition in which a married couple finds it difficult to generate offspring. The deficiency may lie with the husband or the wife. In many cases the condition can be cured. Sterility does not nullify a marriage. Cf. Dr. Carlo Rizzo, s.v. "Sterility," in Roberti and Palazzini, pp. 1163-1165.

10. This does not include artificial means of birth control, where a deliberate attempt is made to prevent conception. This deliberate, artificial circumvention of the conjugal act's purpose is sinful.

11. Congregation for the Doctrine of the Faith, *Considerations Regarding Proposals to Give Legal Recognition to Unions Between Homosexual Persons*, no. 7. (Footnotes omitted throughout.) Hereafter referenced as *Considerations*. This document is available at www.vatican.va/roman_curia/congregations/cfaith/documents/rc_con_cfaith_doc_20030731_homosexual-unions_en.html.

"THE CHURCH ALLOWS A STERILE COUPLE TO MARRY FOR PURPOSES OF MUTUAL SUPPORT, SO TWO HOMOSEXUALS SEEKING MUTUAL SUPPORT SHOULD ALSO BE ALLOWED TO MARRY!"

Mutual support is one of marriage's secondary ends and a marriage is valid when contracted for any one of its ends, provided it remains open to the possibility of procreation.[12] Pope Pius XI teaches:

> Both matrimony and the use of the matrimonial right have secondary ends—such as mutual help, the fostering of reciprocal love, and the abatement of concupiscence—which husband and wife are quite entitled to have in view, so long as the intrinsic nature of that act, and therefore its due subordination to its primary end, is safeguarded.[13]

Since a homosexual couple is incapable of performing the conjugal act and assuring marriage's primary end, their union cannot be matrimonial. And so, the mutual help of two homosexuals cannot be conjugal but only that of friends.

"TO FORBID HOMOSEXUALS TO MARRY IS DISCRIMINATION!"

It is not discrimination. "The denial of the social and legal status of marriage to forms of cohabitation that are not and cannot be marital is not opposed to justice; on the contrary, justice requires it."[14]

---

12. Cf. Pietro Palazzini, s.v. "Marriage" in Roberti and Palazzini, p. 732.
13. Pius XI, Encyclical *Casti Conubii*, the monks of Solesmes, eds., *Papal Teachings—Matrimony* (Boston: St. Paul Editions, 1963), p. 250, no. 319.
14. *Considerations*, no. 8.

"IT IS UNJUST NOT TO ALLOW HOMOSEXUALS TO MARRY ONE ANOTHER, FORCING THEM TO PRACTICE CHASTITY UNWILLINGLY!"

As Saint Paul teaches, the unchaste will not enter the Kingdom of Heaven.[15] Everyone is obliged to practice chastity according to his state in life. This obligation proceeds from natural ethics and revealed morals and the Church cannot change this. Married spouses must live chastely in observance of matrimonial fidelity, and the unmarried must live chastely, abstaining from sexual intercourse.

If a person lacks the physical, psychological or other conditions to contract matrimony, he must practice perfect chastity in celibacy. Not only is there glory in choosing celibacy out of love for the Kingdom of Heaven, there is also merit in accepting the chastity that circumstances impose as a means of subjecting oneself to God's holy will.

---

15. Eph. 5:5; 1 Cor. 6:9-10; 15:50; Gal. 5:19-21; Col. 3:5-6.

CHAPTER 13
The Romantic Myth and the Tragic Reality

The homosexual movement spins a glamorous, romantic vision of its lifestyle, which is faithfully echoed by the entertainment industry and liberal media. Hollywood presents homosexuals and lesbians as young, good-looking, healthy and radiating happiness. Likewise, homosexual partners are presented as romantic and successful.

This screen image is in stark contrast with the tragic reality.

A ROMANTIC MYTH...

Sr. Joan Chittister, a radical dissident nun who has long campaigned for women priests, appears to subscribe to this Hollywood model. Writing in the *National Catholic Reporter*, she waxes poetic when contrasting two couples and their children:

> Every week I see them go down the aisle to Communion, the parents teaching all the way: "Fold your hands. Like this." "Hold your hand out straight for the priest." The children are about 7 and 8 now. The little boy cranes his neck out of his stiff shirt. The little girl touches the bow in her hair lightly, lovingly, her light cotton skirt swishing as she walks. They all receive Communion every Sunday. You can see the delight on the children's faces as they come back up the aisle. You can hear their parents' pride in them at the coffee klatch after Mass.
>
> The parents are professional people who couldn't conceive, so they adopted two minority children. They only intended to take the boy but, when they saw his little sister, they couldn't bear to separate them. It's a joy to watch them grow. It is a "Catholic Family of the Year" vignette.

In contrast to this perfect, loving couple, she presents another. The woman is on her third husband and has three children. These youngsters have nothing: "No clothes, no training, no religion, no love." Sister Chittister concludes: "Neither vignette is fictional. Both of them involve real people in real places. The second couple is heterosexual; the first couple is gay."[1]

Despite mentioning "real people" and "real places," Sister Chittister loses touch with the real world when she contrasts these couples and their children. They are neither valid nor typical samples. Such an idyllic depiction is all too common among those who believe in revolutionary utopias and who, in this case, see the world through the prism of a homosexual ideology.

...AND THE TRAGIC REALITY

The tragic truth is that this romantic image of homosexual "love" contrasts with reality. Behind the cheerful veneer, the homosexual lifestyle is fraught with violence, infidelity and trauma.

The cold hard facts prove that erotic (and neurotic) sentimentality between people of the same sex has nothing of the conjugal love uniting a man and a woman in legitimate traditional marriage contracted in accordance with God's plan and natural law. No amount of window dressing can veil the truth.

AN UNWANTED "MONOGAMY"

If homosexuality is to be accepted as normal, it needs to appear like heterosexuality. For this reason, the homosexual movement creates the myth of homosexual "monogamy"[2]

---

1. Sr. Joan Chittister, "Pondering Premises that Some Things Cause Confusion Among the Faithful," *National Catholic Reporter*, Aug. 27, 1999, www.natcath.org/NCR_Online/archives2/1999c/082799/082799n.htm.
2. From an etymological perspective, the word *monogamy* should only be used for true marriage. (From Late Latin *monogamia*, from Greek, *monogamos*, monogamous, from *mon-* + *gamos* marriage, from *gamein* to marry.) For this reason, when referring to homosexual relationships we use quotes.

where stable "couples" keep a matrimonial-like "fidelity" similar to that of true marriage.

However, a relationship based on deviated sentiment and tendency cannot create the conditions for fidelity found in true monogamous marriage. The few homosexual partners who maintain stable links are exceptions. Moreover, stability in the homosexual world does not mean fidelity.

Indeed, the "monogamy" myth runs contrary to the homosexual experience. In a study of young Dutch homosexuals, Dr. Maria Xiridou of the Amsterdam Municipal Health Service reported that relationships on the average last between 1-1½ years. She also reported that each homosexual had on average eight other partners per year besides the "stable" one.[3]

The fact is that many homosexuals do not cherish "monogamy." Dr. Barry Adam, a homosexual professor at Canada's University of Windsor, presented the results of his study of sixty homosexual couples at an August 2003 meeting of the American Sociological Association. "A slim 25 percent of [homosexuals] interviewed reported being monogamous," Dr. Adam commented.

> Those that were monogamous were more likely to be younger, more likely to be in newer, shorter relationships…. One of the reasons I think younger men tend to start with the vision of monogamy is because they are coming with a heterosexual script in their head and are applying it to relationships with men. What they don't see is that the gay community has their own order and own ways that seem to work better.[4]

---

3. Maria Xiridou, et al., "The contribution of steady and casual partnerships to the incidence of HIV infection among homosexual men in Amsterdam," *AIDS*, (2003) 17(7), p. 1031.

4. Ryan Lee, "Gay Couples Likely to Try Non-Monogamy," *New York Blade*, www.nyblade.com/2003/8-22/news/national/nonmonog.cfm.

Lesbian activist Brenda Schumacher affirms that "not all lesbians are interested in monogamy or serial monogamy."[5]

Psychologist Gerard van den Aardweg states: "Homosexual restlessness cannot be appeased, much less so by having one partner, because these persons are propelled by an insatiable pining for the *unattainable* fantasy figure."[6]

MAKING THE MARQUIS DE SADE
"LOOK LIKE A RED CROSS NURSE"

Marshall Kirk and Hunter Madsen state: "Gay men tend to bring to their relationship a raft of misconceptions, neuroses, and unrealistic expectations, and burden their love affairs past the point that they can handle."[7]

Nor could it be otherwise in a relationship based on an unnatural and disorderly passion of the flesh. As Saint Paul teaches: "Now the works of the flesh are obvious: immorality, impurity, licentiousness, idolatry, sorcery, hatreds, rivalry, jealousy, outbursts of fury, acts of selfishness, dissensions, factions, occasions of envy, drinking bouts, orgies, and the like."[8]

Kirk and Madsen shed some insight on how well Saint Paul's words fit the homosexual world: "The gay bar is the arena of sexual competition, and it brings out all that is most loathsome in human nature. Here, stripped of the façade of wit and cheer, gays stand nakedly revealed as single-minded, selfish sexual predators...and enact vignettes of contempt and cruelty that

---

5. Rex Wockner, "Sex-Lib Activists Confront 'Sex Panic,'" *Pink Ink*, Dec. 1997, Vol. 1, no. 3, www.khsnet.net/pinkink/vol1-3/sexlib.htm.

6. van den Aardweg, p. 62. (Emphasis in the original.)

7. Kirk and Madsen, p. 320. Similar observations have been made by specialists. Cf. Gerard J.M. van den Aardweg, pp. 53-57, and Joseph Nicolosi, *Reparative Therapy of Male Homosexuality* (Northvale, N.J.: Jason Aronson, Inc., 1997), pp. 109-123.

8. Gal. 5:19-21.

make the Comte de Sade look like a Red Cross nurse."[9]

A PROMISCUOUS INFERNO

The promiscuity of the homosexual lifestyle borders on the unimaginable. Statistics, homosexual memoirs and biographies all point to promiscuity with abysmal social and public health consequences.[10]

The problems start with perception. Homosexuals simply do not see promiscuity as harmful. In the words of homosexual writer Lars Eighner: "I see nothing wrong with gay promiscuity. I think it is one of the most positive aspects of gay life that people of very different circumstances can achieve intimacy very quickly."[11]

Thomas E. Schmidt, director of the Westminster Institute, Santa Barbara, notes that "promiscuity among homosexual men is not a mere stereotype, and it is not merely the majority experience—it is virtually the only experience."[12]

Social scientists Robert T. Michael, John H. Gagnon, Edward O. Laumann and Gina Kolata carried out an extensive survey on American sexual behavior and published their work in 1994. The authors comment on the investigations done by the Centers for Disease Control and Prevention in 1982, when AIDS first appeared, and conclude: "Gay men with AIDS

9.   Kirk and Madsen, p. 313. The notorious Donatien Alphonse François, Comte de Sade, better known as the Marquis de Sade (1740-1814), was an impious libertine whose writings mix sexual aberrations with blasphemies and sacrileges. His practice of torturing prostitutes for his own sexual pleasure gave rise to the word *sadism*.

10. Cf. Alan P. Bell and Martin S. Weinberg, *Homosexualities: A Study of Diversity Among Men and Women* (New York: Simon & Shuster, 1978); "Resurgent Bacterial Sexually Transmitted Disease Among Men Who Have Sex With Men—King County, Washington, 1997-1999," *Morbidity and Mortality Weekly Report*, Sept. 10, 1999, Vol. 48, no. 35, pp. 773-777.

11. Lars Eighner, "Why I Write Gay Erotica," www.io.com/~eighner/works/essays/why_i_write_gay_erotica.html.

12. Thomas E. Schmidt, *Straight & Narrow? Compassion & Clarity in the Homosexuality Debate* (Downers Grove, Ill.: InterVarsity Press, 1995), p. 108.

interviewed in the early 1980's reported they had on average 1,100 partners in their lifetimes and some had had many more."[13]

The AIDS epidemic has not stopped homosexual promiscuity. On October 15, 2003, a coalition of individuals, community leaders and service providers addressing the health needs of homosexual and bisexual men in Seattle and King County, Washington, published *A Community Manifesto: A New Response to HIV and STDs*. The document affirms:

> In the face of alarming increases in HIV and STD infection rates among Gay, Bisexual, and other men who have sex with men, we—the MSM HIV/STD Prevention Task Force—issue this **Manifesto** calling for desperately needed community norms and actions. **Gay, Bisexual, and other men who have sex with men must act against the behaviors and attitudes responsible for the increased spread of these diseases.** Today one in seven Gay, Bisexual, and other men who have sex with men are infected with HIV. Among Gay men in King County, syphilis rates are 100 times higher than in the general heterosexual population, and are estimated to be 1000 times higher among HIV positive Gay men than among the general heterosexual population. These rates show we have stopped doing the things that protect us and our sex partners from needless infection.[14]

HIGHER RATES OF "DOMESTIC VIOLENCE"

The homosexual lifestyle is also characterized by higher rates of domestic violence.

---

13. Robert T. Michael, et al., *Sex in America: A Definitive Survey* (Boston: Little, Brown and Co., 1994), p. 209.

14. *A Community Manifesto: A New Response to HIV and STDs*, www.metrokc.gov/health/apu/taskforce/manifesto.htm. (Emphasis in the original.)

Perhaps influenced by Hollywood's spin, lesbian psychotherapist Kali Munro writes: "When I first heard about violence in lesbian relationships, I found it hard to believe. It did not fit my idealized image of the lesbian community."[15]

Indeed, many homosexual relationships are far from being Sister Chittister's "Catholic Family of the Year." Numerous authors document the violence among homosexual and lesbian partners.[16] A study published in December 2002 in the *American Journal of Public Health* concluded:

> Rates of battering victimization among urban MSM [Men who have Sex with Men] are substantially higher than among heterosexual men and possibly heterosexual women. Public health efforts directed toward addressing intimate partner battering among these men are needed.[17]

HIGHER ALCOHOL AND DRUG ABUSE

Higher rates of alcohol and drug abuse are also reported. Dr. Schmidt provides significant findings:

> A Boston study found that, for the years 1985-1988, 80 percent of 481 homosexual men had used marijuana... 60 percent cocaine, 30 percent amphetamines and 20 percent LSD. A 1988-1989 Canadian study found that 76.3 percent of 612 male homosexual subjects regularly used alcohol, 32.2 percent tobacco, and 45.6 percent at least one drug. A national study of 1,924 female

15. Kali Munro, "Talking About Lesbian Partner Abuse," *Siren*, Oct/Nov. 1998, www.kalimunro.com/article_partnerabuse.html.

16. Cf. www.lib.jjay.cuny.edu/research/DomesticViolence/v.html.

17. Gregory L. Greenwood et al., "Battering Victimization Among a Probability-Based Sample of Men Who Have Sex With Men," in *American Journal of Public Health*, Dec. 2002, Vol. 92, No. 12, pp. 1964-1969.

homosexuals conducted in 1984 found that 83 percent regularly used alcohol…47 percent smoked marijuana, and 30 percent regularly smoked tobacco.

Whenever these studies consider connections, they show a direct correlation between the number of partners, drug use and the likelihood of unsafe sex.[18]

This higher rate of alcohol and drug abuse by homosexuals has not diminished. Between October 15, 2002 and January 15, 2003, a total of 319 organizations and individuals responded to the British Government's request for submission papers on alcohol misuse.[19] In her paper, on behalf of the Lancashire, U.K., organization Lesbian Information Service, Jan Bridget submitted an overview of U.S. research on this issue:

> Early US research indicated alcohol/drug misuse was higher among lesbians and gays than amongst the heterosexual population….
>
> Some of the early research has been challenged by Paul, Stall & Bloomfield (1991) who cited opportunistic sampling techniques (i.e. bar-patrons who are more likely to abuse alcohol) in their critique. Two later studies, Bloomfield (1993) and McKiernan & Peterson (1993) both found that lesbian alcohol abuse in the Chicago and San Francisco areas was no higher than that of heterosexual women.
>
> More recent studies,[20] however, have again found higher levels of use and abuse….
>
> For several years now there have been large-scale studies conducted with high-school students in some areas of the

---

18. Thomas E. Schmidt, p. 111.
19. Prime Minister's Strategy Unit, "Responses to the Alcohol Misuse Consultation Paper," www.number-10.gov.uk/output/Page4490.asp#L.
20. Jan Bridget cites the following: Skinner and Otis (1996); Abbott (1998); Jaffe, Clance, Nichols and Emshoff (2000); Diamant, et al. (2000).

USA (83,000 Youth, 2000). These have consistently found higher levels of abuse (both alcohol and drugs) among LGB young people than among heterosexual youth.[21]

AIDS AND SEXUALLY TRANSMITTED DISEASES

Rampant homosexual promiscuity is an ongoing concern among the medical community as it tries to contain the growing numbers of people infected with HIV/AIDS and other sexually transmitted diseases.

In July 2002, the Gay and Lesbian Medical Association published a news release with health issues of special concern to homosexuals. The release observed:

> Sexually transmitted diseases occur in sexually active gay men at a high rate. This includes STD infections for which effective treatment is available (syphilis, gonorrhea, chlamydia, pubic lice, and others), and for which no cure is available (HIV, Hepatitis A, B, or C virus, Human Papilloma Virus, etc.).[22]

According to the Centers for Disease Control and Prevention, the estimated total of adult AIDS cases in the country by December 2002 was 877,275. Of this number, a total of 496,354 adults, or 57 percent, have died. The breakdown of these 877,275 cases by exposure category shows that 420,790 cases, or 48 percent, result from male-to-male sexual contact. Another 59,719 cases, or 7 percent, result from a combination of male-to-male sexual contact and injection drug use.[23] Considering the fact that homosexual men make up less than three percent of the

21. Jan Bridget, for Lesbian Information Services, "Alcohol/Drug Misuse," www.number-10.gov.uk/su/alcohol/submissions/lesbian.pdf.
22. "Ten Things Gay Men Should Discuss with Their Health Care Providers," www.glma.org/news/releases/n02071710gaythings.html.
23. Cf. www.cdc.gov/hiv/stats.htm.

male population, the disproportion is glaring.

In its publication "A Glance at the HIV Epidemic," the CDC states: "By risk, men who have sex with men (MSM) represent the largest proportion of new infections." The bulletin also estimates that 60% of all new AIDS infections each year result from male-to-male sexual contact.[24]

The medical community's concern grew with the CDC's July 2003 observation that the number of new AIDS cases per year is on the rise again in the United States.[25]

DEALING WITH SUICIDE

Severe depression and suicidal thoughts and attempts are also more frequent among homosexuals, especially when young, than among the general population. Study after study come up with consistent results.

In December 1999, the National Institute of Mental Health reported:

> With regard to suicide attempts, several state and national studies have reported that high school students who report to be homosexually and bisexually active have higher rates of suicide thoughts and attempts in the past year compared to youth with heterosexual experience.[26]

In their 1997 study of 750 males between 18-27 years of age, Christopher Bagley and Pierre Tremblay report:

> Significant higher rates of previous suicidal ideas and actions were reported by homosexually oriented

---

24. www.cdc.gov/nchstp/od/news/At-a-Glance.pdf
25. Cf. www.cdc.gov/hiv/stats/hasr1402/commentary.htm.
26. "Frequently Asked Questions about Suicide," National Institute of Mental Health, www.nimh.nih.gov/research/suicidefaq.cfm.

males accounting for 62.5% of suicide attempters. These findings, which indicate that homosexual and bisexual males are 13.9 times more at risk for a serious suicide attempt, are consonant with previous findings.[27]

PLAYING WITH FIRE

These facts prove that the analogy between homosexual partnership and traditional marriage is baseless. Higher rates of violence, disease and suicide are indicative of a lifestyle that puts its tragic victims at high risk. Indeed, those who enter this highly promiscuous and restless world are playing with fire.

---

27. Christopher Bagley and Pierre Tremblay, "Suicidal behaviors in homosexual and bisexual males," *Crisis* (1997), Vol. 1, pp. 24-34. Quote is from the abstract by the authors available at www.virtualcity.com/youthsuicide/gbsuicide1.htm.

CHAPTER 14
A False Concept of Compassion

In an effort to gain acceptance, the homosexual movement often frames the debate around "compassion." Thus, anyone favoring the homosexual agenda shows compassion, while those opposing it show none.

Undoubtedly, compassion is among the most beautiful and ennobling sentiments. It reveals selflessness, disinterestedness and love of one's neighbor. Etymologically, compassion means *to suffer together*.[1] Thus, compassion is a deep awareness of another's suffering, coupled with the desire to alleviate it.

Psychologically, compassion stems from the fact that all men share the same human nature. As the ancient playwright Terence wrote: "I am a man, and nothing relating to men is a matter of indifference to me."[2]

MANIPULATING A NOBLE SENTIMENT

Like everything on earth, this noble sentiment can also be deformed and misused. The homosexual movement did just this, hijacking this word and using it as an emotional label.

A typical example is a press statement by the Rainbow Sash Movement USA (National Organization of Gay/Lesbian/Bisexual/Transgender Catholics) attacking the document *Considerations Regarding Proposals to Give Legal Recognition to Unions Between Homosexual Persons*, released by the Congregation for the Doctrine of the Faith on July 31, 2003. After scolding the Vatican for its "hysteria," the press release concludes:

> Furthermore, the Vatican appears determined to

---

1. Latin *compassio*, sympathy, from *compassus*, past participle of *compati*, to feel pity: *com*, together + *pati*, to suffer.
2. Publius Terentius Afer, *Self Tormentor*—Act I: *Homo sum: humani nil a me alienum puto.*

end up on the wrong side of compassion on the issue of homosexual relationships. The ugly language and the hurtful pejorative tone used about gay marriages, such as "deviant behavior," "gravely immoral" unions and the "legalization of evil" speaks of [a] Papacy that has lost its moral compass.[3]

In a commentary about the Vatican's *Considerations, National Catholic Reporter* publisher Tom Fox writes: "Instead of white heat, judgment and absolute demands, wouldn't the Roman prelates have more influence if they posed questions in a spirit of compassion?"[4]

Lack of compassion was also the main argument of Charles Cox, then executive director of Dignity USA, commenting on the Vatican's 1999 banning of Fr. Robert Nugent and Sr. Jeannine Gramick's heterodox outreach to homosexuals and lesbians: "This is certainly going to put a great deal of pressure on diocesan ministries—pressure to absolutely conform to Church teaching, with no room for compassion or understanding of lesbian and gay people."[5]

COMPASSION IS SUPPOSEDLY NON-JUDGMENTAL

Such statements reflect a false understanding of compassion. At the heart of this misconception is the erroneous idea that compassion is based on emotion alone. Any involvement of reason, and especially moral judgment, supposedly destroys compassion.

From this mistaken perspective, compassion towards one's neighbor focuses exclusively on eliminating needs or alleviating

3. "National Gay Catholic Organization Responds to the Vatican's Smoke and Mirrors Document," Rainbow Sash Movement USA, Aug. 2, 2003, www.biz.yahoo.com/prnews/030802/nysa010_1.html.
4. Tom Fox, "Gays Get Hit Twice," *National Catholic Reporter*, Aug. 7, 2003.
5. Teresa Malcolm, "Pair Dealt a Lifetime Ban on Ministry to Homosexuals," *National Catholic Reporter*, July 30, 1999.

suffering. However, if this suffering is caused by sinful behavior, as in the case of homosexuality, then compassion consists in showing acceptance of this behavior, not rejection. Hence, this liberal compassion is "inclusive," "all embracing" and "non-judgmental."

Unitarian minister Tom Goldsmith offers an explanation of this non-judgmental compassion. His first example is the late Cardinal O'Connor, since he was the first to open Catholic hospitals to AIDS victims. However, the cardinal's compassion was diminished by the fact that "he still held to be true, God's condemnation of homosexuals." In this case, Goldsmith observes, "judgment remains the ultimate barrier to empathy and genuine (divine?) understanding among people." His second example presents "a powerful demonstration in the art of non-judgmental behavior," that of a Massachusetts high school student who, with the help of the faculty advisor for the school's Gay-Straight Alliance, led a successful campaign promoting acceptance of a homosexual football teammate. Goldsmith concludes: "Maybe that's what compassion really means: walking through the real world with eyes open and owning a heart free of any judgments."[6]

COMPASSION MUST BE GUIDED
BY REASON, NOT SENTIMENT

This non-judgmental compassion is both false and absurd, for it is a subversion of true compassion.

Saint Thomas Aquinas teaches that the sentiment of compassion only becomes a virtue when it is guided by reason, since "it is essential to human virtue that the movements of the soul should be regulated by reason."[7] Without this regulation,

---

6. Tom Goldsmith, "Reverendly Yours," *The Torch*, May 11, 2000, www.slcuu.org/torch/1999-00/05-11-00.pdf.

7. St.Thomas Aquinas, *Summa Theologica*, II-II, q. 30, c. 3.

compassion is only a passion. Like all passions, compassion in this case is a powerful but irrational inclination, and therefore a potentially dangerous one since it can favor not only good, but also evil.[8] To feel pity at the sight of someone's sufferings is normal. However, to act without prudent analysis may lead to unintended harm.

Consider, for example, the case of a man who buys whiskey for his friend—an alcoholic—because he cannot bear to see him suffer when going without a drink. Likewise, consider a father who plies his gambling-addicted son with cash because he is distressed at the thought that the son suffers at not being able to gamble. His action does not show true love for his son. Instead of helping his son free himself from gambling's stranglehold, he supports the vice with easy access to money.

HELPING VICE IS NOT COMPASSION

While everything must be done to help sinners, this cannot include helping them sin or remain in vice. Given human frailty, a sinner deserves pity and compassion. However, vice and sin must be excluded from this compassion, since sin can never be the proper object of compassion.[9]

When a misguided pity leads to supplying the sinner with the means to remain attached to his vice, this assistance, be it material or moral, actually helps keep the sinner chained to his evil ways. Such action helps the vice, not the person. Despite good intentions, the action is harmful.

True compassion leads a sinner away from vice and back to virtue. As Saint Thomas explains:

> We love sinners out of charity, not so as to will
> what they will, or to rejoice in what gives them joy,

---

8. Ibid., II-II, q. 30, a. 1, ad 3.
9. Ibid., II-II, q. 30, a. 1, ad 1.

but so as to make them will what we will, and rejoice in what rejoices us. Hence it is written: "They shall be turned to thee, and thou shalt not be turned to them (Jer. 15:19)."[10]

The Divine example is that of the Good Shepherd who goes after the stray sheep to bring it back to the fold. Another moving example is Saint Monica, mother of Saint Augustine. She never endorsed her son's impure lifestyle and heretical beliefs, but she also never stopped praying and working towards his conversion. "A mother's tears" eventually did convert him and he became one of the greatest Catholic luminaries of all time.

TRUE COMPASSION STEMS FROM CHARITY

True compassion is an effect of charity.[11] However, the object of this virtue is God, whose love extends to creatures.[12] Hence the virtue of compassion seeks to bring God to the one who suffers and make him participate in God's infinite love.

Saint Augustine expresses this very beautifully:

> "Thou shalt love thy neighbor as thyself." Now, you love yourself suitably when you love God better than yourself. What, then, you aim at in yourself you must aim at in your neighbor, namely, that he may love God with a perfect affection.[13]

Thus, while commiserating with another's sufferings, love of neighbor must always be for the love of God.

---

10. Ibid. II-II, q. 25, a. 6, ad 4.
11. Ibid. II-II, q. 30, a. 3, ad 3.
12. Ibid. II-II, q. 25, a. 3.
13. St. Augustine, *Of the Morals of the Catholic Church*, no. 49, www.newadvent.org/fathers/1401.htm.

THE MANIPULATION OF
COMPASSION MUST BE DENOUNCED

To speak of "non-judgmental" compassion is a contradiction in terms since it denies the fundamental role of reason and morality. It is just one more artifice employed by the homosexual movement in this Cultural War where words and concepts become real weapons.

From a Catholic and rational standpoint, compassion is only true when it aims at the real good of one's neighbor. This good consists, above all, in his eternal salvation but also encompasses alleviating his temporal sufferings. To assist him to remain in vice and sin out of a misguided pity for his temporal sufferings is to ignore his spiritual welfare and salvation. There can be no greater cruelty.

CHAPTER 15
Refuting Revisionist Biblical Scholars—Sodom Was Punished for Its Homosexuality

Among the tactics outlined in their book, *After the Ball*, Marshall Kirk and Hunter Madsen include muddying the waters of religion. They suggest casting liberal against traditional teachings, thus shattering unified religious opposition to homosexuality.

One major problem is that the Biblical record against homosexuality is very clear and categorical. The only way around this obstacle is to find theologians and writers influenced by the homosexual ideology who can find interpretations that muddy the crystalline waters of the Faith.

WAS SODOM PUNISHED FOR INHOSPITALITY?

It has always been known that Sodom and Gomorrah were chastised with fire from Heaven because of the sin of homosexuality.

In more recent times, however, certain Protestant and Catholic commentators, when not denying it altogether, play down this notion. Such commentators change the focus of the chastisement from sodomy to other sins which the Bible says the inhabitants of those cities also committed: rape, violence, lack of mercy, injustice, idolatry and even lack of hospitality. In this way, they dilute or deny the special gravity of unnatural vice as one of the "sins that cry out to heaven for vengeance."[1]

---

1. "Since the sixteenth century, it has been the custom to apply the term 'sins that cry to heaven for vengeance' to certain faults that gravely violate the social order, and which Sacred Scripture expressly says cry to heaven for vengeance, i.e. call down God's punishment on those who commit them. There are four such sins: homicide (Gen. 4:10); sodomy (Gen.19:13); oppression of widows and orphans (Exod. 22:22ff.); depriving workers of their just wage (Deut. 24:17ff.; James 5:4)" (Dom Gregorio Manise, O.S.B., s.v. "Sins That Cry Out To Heaven For Vengeance," in *Dictionary of Moral Theology* [Westminster, Md.: The Newman Press, 1962], p. 1139).

• *THE NEW DICTIONARY OF THEOLOGY*

One example of this new focus is the entry for "Homosexuality" in *The New Dictionary of Theology* published in 1987:

> Homosexual activity when encountered or referred in the OT and NT is condemned. Modern biblical scholarship, however, suggests that the condemnation in the OT is often directed against homosexual acts by heterosexual persons, especially when the situation suggests rape (Gen 19, Sodom and Gomorrah), or against acts in a context with idolatrous connotations (Lev 18-22, 20:13, the Leviticus Holiness Code), or which are seen as violations of social justice demands for hospitality (Isa 1:9; Ezek 16:46-51; Jer 23:14). Both male and female homosexual relationships are condemned in a NT citation as an expression of idolatry (Rom 1:25-27) and same-sex genital acts are mentioned among those which violate God's law and exclude the perpetrator from the Kingdom of Heaven (Rom 1:25-27; 1 Cor 69:10; 1 Tm 1:9-10). Most modern exegetes acknowledge the difficulty of determining the precise meaning of these texts and the consequent problem of applying them ethically to condemn homosexuals or their genital acts.[2]

• *HUMAN SEXUALITY: NEW DIRECTIONS IN AMERICAN CATHOLIC THOUGHT*

Another striking example is *Human Sexuality—New Directions in American Catholic Thought*. This 1977 book was commissioned by the Catholic Theological Society of America.

---

2. James A. Komonchak et al., eds., *The New Dictionary of Theology* (Collegeville, Minn.: The Liturgical Press, 1987), p. 490.

In discussing homosexuality, *Human Sexuality* states that the condemnation in Leviticus qualifying it as an "abomination" must be seen in the context of idolatry. "The condemnation of homosexual activity in Leviticus is not an ethical judgment," but rather it is made "on account of its association with idolatry."[3]

Human Sexuality also comments on the destruction of Sodom and Gomorrah: "The Fathers of the Church had no doubt that the nature of the wickedness for which Sodom was punished was the homosexual practice of sodomy."[4] It then compares Sodom's behavior with the collective rape of a traveling Levite's concubine by the inhabitants of Gibeah.[5] It concludes that Sodom and Gomorrah were chastised not because of homosexuality but rather because of rape and inhospitality: "For Sodom as for Gibeah, 'the emphasis falls not on the proposed sexual act per se, but on the terrible violation of the customary law of hospitality.'"[6]

Human Sexuality also lists texts from Sacred Scripture that mention other sins of Sodom and Gomorrah and tries to prove the thesis that Sodom's punishment was not because of homosexuality.[7]

- **THE *NEW AMERICAN BIBLE***

Unfortunately, the commentary on Sodom in the *New American Bible* reflects this same influence. Regarding Genesis 18:20, where God says to Abraham, "The outcry

---

3. Anthony Kosnik et al., *Human Sexuality: New Directions in American Catholic Thought* (New York: Paulist Press, 1977), p. 190. The authors quote from N. H. Snaith, *Leviticus and Numbers*, the Century Bible (London: Nelson, 1967), p. 126.
4. Ibid., p. 191.
5. Judges 19.
6. Kosnik et al., p. 191. The internal quotation is from Anthony Phillips, *Ancient Israel's Criminal Law: A New Approach to the Decalogue* (Oxford: Basil Blackwell, 1970), p. 122.
7. Ibid., pp. 191-196.

against Sodom and Gomorrah is so great, and their sin so grave," the new exegetes comment:

> Israelite tradition was unanimous in ascribing the destruction of Sodom and Gomorrah to the wickedness of these cities, but tradition varied in regard to the nature of this wickedness. According to the present account of the Yahwist, the sin of Sodom was homosexuality (Genesis 19:4-5), which is therefore also known as sodomy; but according to Isaiah (Isaiah 1:9-10; 3:9), it was a lack of social justice; Ezekiel (Ezekiel 16:46-51) described it as a disregard for the poor, whereas Jeremiah (Jeremiah 23:14) saw it as general immorality.[8]

The *New American Bible*'s commentary on Jude 1:7 is another example of this influence. Saint Jude says: "Likewise, Sodom, Gomorrah, and the surrounding towns, which, in the same manner as they, indulged in sexual promiscuity and practiced unnatural vice, serve as an example by undergoing a punishment of eternal fire." The *New American Bible* commentary for this verse reads:

> Practiced unnatural vice: literally, "went after alien flesh." This example derives from Genesis 19:1-25, especially Jude 1:4-11, when the townsmen of Sodom violated both hospitality and morality by demanding that Lot's two visitors (really messengers from Yahweh) be handed over to them so that they could abuse them sexually. **Unnatural vice: this refers to the desire for intimacies by human beings with**

---

8. *New American Bible*, footnote no. 6 to Genesis, Chapter 18, www.usccb.org/nag/bible/genesis/genesis18.htm.

angels (the reverse of the example in Jude 1:6). Sodom (whence "sodomy") and Gomorrah became proverbial object lessons for God's punishment on sin (Isaiah 1:9; Jeremiah 50:40; Amos 4:11; Matthew 10:15; 2 Peter 2:6).[9]

The above are but samples of a revisionist spin on Holy Writ. These revisionists go to great pains to "explain" other passages of the Old and New Testaments, the writings of Church Fathers, Doctors and the condemnations of Popes and councils down through the ages.

SODOM AND GOMORRAH WERE PUNISHED FOR THEIR HOMOSEXUALITY

When analyzing Scripture, these new exegetes generally agree that "the Fathers of the Church had no doubt that the nature of the wickedness for which Sodom was punished was the homosexual practice of sodomy."[10]

Having made this perfunctory bow to Tradition, however, these commentators then turn an about face and affirm the contrary position, based on "modern biblical scholarship" and "the most modern exegetes."

In justifying their denial of Tradition, they claim that further Scriptural passages refer to Sodom's many other sins, and they draw an analogy between the Sodomites' treatment of the two angels and the account of the Gibeah rape in Judges 19.

Their reasoning has no merit.

First of all, the authority of the Church Fathers and Tradition is normative for a Catholic exegete. Secondly, one cannot conclude that the Sodomites' other sins—and not

---

9. *New American Bible*, footnote no. 6 to St. Jude's Epistle, www.usccb.org/nag/bible/jude/jude.htm#v5. (Our emphasis.)
10. Kosnik et al., p. 191.

homosexuality—were what triggered the chastisement. The analogy of the "new exegetes" themselves proves this. In the Gibeah rape of a traveling Levite's concubine, the laws of hospitality and morality were most despicably violated. However, the analogy ends there. Unlike Sodom, Gibeah was not destroyed with sulphurous fire from heaven.[11]

THE FLAWED USE OF OTHER SCRIPTURAL TEXTS

Evidently, such a portentous punishment as the destruction of Sodom and Gomorrah by sulphurous fire is a permanent example for all times,[12] corresponding to an extremely sinful situation. Considering the account in Genesis, there is no doubt that this most grave sin of Sodom was homosexuality.

Since it has been established that the narrative in Genesis is the principal source of information about the sin and chastisement of Sodom and Gomorrah, all other biblical references should be understood in light of this narrative. They complement but do not correct Genesis as the innovators claim.

THE ACCOUNT IN GENESIS

In an anthropomorphic manner, Genesis describes God as if He were a man pondering the chastisement of the two cities:

> Then the Lord said: "The outcry against Sodom and Gomorrah is so great, and their sin so grave, that I must go down and see whether or not their actions fully correspond to the cry against them that comes to Me. I mean to find out."[13]

Next, God sent angels in the form of human pilgrims to

---

11. Gen. 19:23.
12. Deut. 29:23; Isa. 1:9-10; 3:9; 13:19; Jer. 49:18; Lam. 4:6; Amos 4:11; Zeph. 2:9; Matt.10:15; Rom. 9:29; 2 Pet. 2:6; Jude 7.
13. Gen. 18:20-21.

Sodom, where Lot receives them. The narrative continues:

> Before they went to bed, all the townsmen of
> Sodom, both **young and old—all the people** to the
> last man—closed in on the house. They called to Lot
> and said to him, "Where are the **men** who came to
> your house tonight? Bring them out to us that we may
> have **intimacies** with them."[14]

Lot's efforts to reason with the Sodomites came to naught,
so the angels chastised them with blindness. The angels then
said to Lot, "We are about to destroy this place, for the outcry
reaching the Lord against those in the city is so great that He
has sent us to destroy it."[15]

Once Lot and his family had fled, the chastisement came:

> The sun was just rising over the earth as Lot
> arrived in Zoar; at the same time the Lord rained
> down sulphurous fire upon Sodom and Gomorrah
> (from the Lord out of heaven). He overthrew those
> cities and the whole Plain, together with the inhab-
> itants of the cities and the produce of the soil.[16]

THE CORRELATION BETWEEN SINS

The main defect in the false reasoning of the new exegetes
is their failure to consider that one sin is usually related to others,
as either cause or consequence. Just as the heroic practice of
one virtue generally leads to the practice of all the other
virtues, clinging obstinately to one sin allows the sinner to fall
easily into others related by nature or circumstance.

---

14. Gen. 19:4-5.
15. Gen. 19:13.
16. Gen. 19:23-25.

Indeed, the Sodomites did sin by despising the poor and strangers, practicing gluttony and falling into general immorality. However, this does not allow one to conclude that homosexuality is not sinful, as suggested by the *New Dictionary of Theology*. Likewise, it cannot be used to conclude that homosexuality was not the reason for Sodom and Gomorrah's chastisement by fire.

This correlation between sins is contained in the commentary on one of the six verses of Ezechiel (16:46-51) in the *New Dictionary of Theology* and the *New American Bible*. It serves as the basis to conclude that Sodom was punished for "violations of social justice demands for hospitality" and "a disregard for the poor."

Ezechiel 16:49 affirms: "And look at the guilt of your sister Sodom: she and her daughters [neighboring towns influenced by Sodom] were proud, sated with food, complacent in their prosperity, and they gave no help to the poor and needy."[17]

Commenting on this verse, Cornelius a Lapide, one of the greatest Scripture commentators of all time, explains this correlation between sins:

> First [among the vices of Sodom] is pride. Then the satiety of bread, or rather of food, delicacies, banquets. Third, the abundance of goods, of luxury and pleasure. Fourth, idleness. Fifth, lack of mercy....
>
> Hear St. Jerome: "Haughtiness, satiety of bread, the abundance of all things, idleness, pleasures, such were the sins of Sodom. Because of these, they forgot God, since the continual presence of riches seemed perennial and thus there was no need of recourse to God to obtain them." ...Therefore, we first encounter pride in the sins of Sodom. Then God chastises the

---

17. Ezech. 16:49.

proud, permitting them to fall into a great and ignominious lust, as can be deduced from Rom. 1:27....
Also, gluttony led to the downfall of Sodom since it
is the material out of which lust is made. St. Jerome
says: "The lava of the volcanoes of Etna, Vesuvius, or
Olympus do not make the young burn [with lust], but
wine and dainty dishes."...About idleness, St. John
Chrysostom says, "Idleness teaches all malice."

Cornelius a Lapide demonstrates how the Sodomites' lack
of mercy led to the sin of homosexuality:

Fifth, mercilessness, which was the cause of the
lust of the Sodomites: then those who are cruel to
others are also cruel to their own nature, violating the
laws of generation. Those who are cruel to their
neighbor in so far as his sustenance, or even his life,
are also cruel to their own bodies, abusing them
libidinously. Thus the Sodomites who were cruel
towards their guests and the pilgrims—in this case the
angels that had assumed human bodies and presented
themselves as pilgrims to Lot—burned with evil
desires (Gen. 19:5). Lack of mercy and cruelty, therefore, make that those who are cruel respect neither
modesty nor reputation, the body, or the life of their
neighbor, especially that of strangers or pilgrims.
Instead, they treat them as their own, as food for their
lechery—something vile and worthless.[18]

---

18. Cornelius a Lapide, *Commentaria in Scripturam Sacram, Commentaria in
Ezechielem Prophetam* (Paris: Vivès, 1880), Vol. 12, pp. 618-619.

HOMOSEXUALITY HAS NOTHING
TO DO WITH THE ANGELS

As already mentioned, the *New American Bible* commentators of Saint Jude's Epistle claim that Sodom and Gomorrah's practice of "unnatural vice" consisted in "the desire for intimacies by human beings with angels."

The Genesis narrative is clear that the Sodomites believed the two messengers from Yahweh were men: "Where are the men who came to your house tonight? Bring them out to us that we may have intimacies with them."

On the other hand, as the *New American Bible* explains, a literal translation of the Greek original for "practiced unnatural vice" is "went after alien flesh." Thus, the angels' taking on the appearance of human flesh excited the lust of the Sodomites. The Sodomites could not have been sexually attracted to the angelic nature, since this angelic nature was unknown to them. The traditional explanation for "went after alien flesh" is "the pursuit of infamous vices."[19]

Cornelius a Lapide, commenting on the expression "went after alien flesh," quotes Our Lord's words on marriage: "For this reason a man shall leave his father and mother and be joined to his wife, and *the two shall become one flesh*."[20] He explains that two men cannot unite to procreate, and thus "become one flesh." When they unite sexually, therefore, they are "two fleshes," not one, as in marriage. He also explains that it is "alien flesh" because this sexual union is alien to procreation, which is the natural and proper end of the sexual act.[21]

19. Cf. Jose Maria Bover, S.J. and Francisco Cantera Burgos, *Sagrada Biblia: Version Critica Sobre Los Textos Hebreo y Griego* (Madrid: Biblioteca de Autores Cristianos, 1961), p. 1473, fn. 7.
20. Matt. 19:5.
21. Cornelius a Lapide, *Comentaria in Scripturam Sacram*, (Paris: Vivès, 1863), Vol. 20, p. 662.

SODOM AND GOMORRAH COMPOUNDED THEIR HOMOSEXUALITY WITH GREAT INSOLENCE

The insolence of Sodom and Gomorrah amid their sinfulness made the challenge to God even graver. The Prophet Isaiah states this when reprimanding the Jews:

> Jerusalem is crumbling; Judah is falling; for their speech and their deeds are before the Lord, a provocation in the sight of his majesty. Their very look bears witness against them; **their sin like Sodom they vaunt, they hide it not.** Woe to them! They deal out evil to themselves.[22]

LEVITICUS CONDEMNS BOTH IDOLATRY AND HOMOSEXUALITY

Human Sexuality argues that homosexuality is not condemned by Leviticus since "the condemnation of homosexual activity in Leviticus is not an ethical judgment." The condemnation was made "on account of its association with idolatry."

In this passage, the book of Leviticus echoes the Ten Commandments. The Decalogue condemns not only idolatry, but also homosexuality: Idolatry is a fault against the First Commandment and homosexuality a sin against the Sixth.[23] Therefore, unless one sustains the preposterous concept that the Ten Commandments are not an ethical code, a summary of the revealed moral law, there is no basis to affirm that this condemnation of homosexuality "is not an ethical judgment."

Moreover, the context of the condemnation of homosexuality in Leviticus clearly demonstrates that it is based on ethics. The exegetes usually call this part of Leviticus the "Code of Holiness" because it gives practical norms for perfection. It

---

22. Isa. 3:8-9.
23. Exod. 20:1-17; Deut. 5:6-21.

specifically deals with sexual morals and condemns all forms of incest, promiscuity and other forms of sexual aberrations like homosexuality and bestiality.

This is the context of the verse misinterpreted by *Human Sexuality*:

> You shall not have carnal relations with your neighbor's wife, defiling yourself with her.
>
> You shall not offer any of your offspring to be immolated to Moloch, thus profaning the name of your God. I am the LORD.
>
> **You shall not lie with a male as with a woman; such a thing is an abomination.**
>
> You shall not have carnal relations with an animal, defiling yourself with it; nor shall a woman set herself in front of an animal to mate with it; such things are abhorrent.
>
> Do not defile yourselves by any of these things by which the nations whom I am driving out of your way have defiled themselves.
>
> Because their land has become defiled, I am punishing it for its wickedness, by making it vomit out its inhabitants.[24]

The text is clear: Do not follow in the footsteps of idolatrous people who sacrificed their children to idols and committed abominations like homosexuality and bestiality.

These norms for holiness are similar to those Saint Paul gave the Corinthians:

> Do you not know that the unjust will not inherit the kingdom of God? Do not be deceived; neither

24. Lev. 18:20-25.

fornicators, nor idolaters, nor adulterers, nor boy prostitutes, nor practicing homosexuals, nor thieves, nor the greedy, nor drunkards, nor slanderers, nor robbers will inherit the kingdom of God.[25]

HOMOSEXUALITY: A SIN THAT CRIES OUT TO HEAVEN FOR VENGEANCE

Homosexuality is ranked among the "sins that cry to heaven for vengeance." Scripture explicitly states this when the angels said to Lot: "We are about to destroy this place, for the outcry reaching the Lord against those in the city is so great that he has sent us to destroy it."

The special gravity of the sin of homosexuality is due to the fact that it violates the natural order of the sexes established by God in creation.

In his Second Epistle, Saint Peter shows how the punishment of Sodom and Gomorrah remains as a warning to evildoers: "God condemned the cities of Sodom and Gomorrah (to destruction), reducing them to ashes, making them an example for the godless (people) of what is coming."[26]

Thus, it is clear that, even though the inhabitants of Sodom and Gomorrah committed various interrelated sins, the sin of homosexuality was the cause of the divine chastisement. This is the unanimous interpretation of the Fathers of the Church and all traditional exegetes. Explanations contrary to this tradition do violence to the sacred texts.

Hence, it is fitting to remember Pope Saint Celestine's warning to the clergy of Gaul: "*Desinat incessere novitas vetustatem*"—Let novelty cease to attack antiquity![27]

---

25. 1 Cor. 6:9-10.
26. 2 Pet. 2:6.
27. Letter from Pope St. Celestine to the clergy of Gaul—431. Quoted by John Chapman, O.S.B., s.v. "Fathers of the Church," in *The Catholic Encyclopedia* (1913), Vol. 6, p. 2.

PART III
Natural Law and Church Teaching Have Always Condemned Homosexuality

CHAPTER 16
Natural Law:
Man's Necessary Point of Reference

The homosexual movement tries to impose a false morality on society. This pseudo-morality is based on the philosophical premise that objective moral norms do not exist and the individual's choice alone should determine human behavior.

Proponents of the movement put a *democratic* spin on a true statement. Indeed, man must follow his conscience. However, this does not mean that each and every individual is free to choose as he well pleases.

MORALITY IS NOT THE FRUIT OF "DEMOCRATIC CONSENSUS"

All too often, people confuse democracy as a form of government with a kind of democratic consensus that determines the norms of human thought and conduct in society.

Thus something is good or bad, true or false, beautiful or ugly, based on public opinion as expressed in referenda or opinion polls. In morals, as in politics, everyone is expected to accept the will of the majority, even if they personally disagree.

Morality thus becomes the result of the sum of individual opinions, and everyone must submit to the collective expression of the majority.

Though this way of thinking may be attractive at first glance, it is nevertheless misleading.

THE NEED FOR A SUPREME LEGISLATOR

If the moral law were not inscribed in human nature and present in man's conscience, the dictates of positive law would not resonate in his soul. No relation would exist between laws and man's innermost being. Laws would be purely external impositions, only to be obeyed because of the State's coercive power.

Thus, laws opposing man's rational nature would be totally arbitrary, since they would reflect the whims and fancies of lawmakers. This would not be true law, and it would not be binding in conscience.

Furthermore, law based exclusively on human volition carries no moral authority over man, since, from a natural point of view, the will of one man is as good as that of another. No man's will is *naturally* superior to his fellowman's will. Therefore, this volitional law would also not be binding on man's conscience.

For a law to bind man's conscience, its deepest roots and ultimate guarantee must be found in a Supreme Legislator, whose Will is naturally superior to human will.[1] This superior Will must belong to God because His alone is superior to all other wills. This Supreme Will is expressed both in positive laws, i.e., laws established by God and contained in Revelation, and in natural law, as expressed throughout Creation.

THE EXISTENCE AND EFFECTIVENESS OF NATURAL LAW

Anyone can observe that the universe is ruled by unchanging laws: Leaves are green; blood is red; water freezes at a given temperature; birds fly; night follows day; and so on. Moreover, centuries of experience show that it has always been like this and that it always will be so, independent of man's will. All these things are dictated by the very nature of things. The nature of things determines their end, moves them towards it and grants them the means necessary to achieve it.

Indeed, after creating the universe from nothing, God did

---

1. Cf. Fr. Charles Coppens, S.J., *A Brief Text-Book of Moral Philosophy*, revised by Fr. Henry S. Spalding, S.J. (New York: Shwartz, Kirwin and Fauss, 1924), pp. 62-63.

not abandon His creatures to chance and leave them without purpose or guidance. On the contrary, He ordered and directed them to an end according to the plan established by His Divine Wisdom.

The very nature God gave inanimate creatures governs them. These laws that govern inanimate Creation are called "natural physical laws" or "the laws of nature." These natural physical laws govern the workings of the physical universe. Laws like "substances expand when heated" and "the earth revolves around the sun" express the constant, invariable rules that physical things follow. It is only proper that natural physical laws be constant and invariable and brook no exceptions. Thus, if a natural physical law failed to work even once, it would no longer be law.

In an ordered universe guided by understandable physical laws, man also must have a final end and moral laws tailored to his nature that guide and govern him. It would be absurd if such ordering laws existed but were not easily knowable by man.

A moment's reflection suffices to conclude that such laws exist and that man, too, is subject to the supreme order God established in Creation.

Man's sense of being tells him that he is a man and a human being. His reason concludes that he exists within the limits of human nature. He knows that he is not a rock or a plant or a mere animal. He also knows he is not an angel but a man. Human nature is the "blueprint" for man's conduct as a human being.

Part of the law governing man refers to non-free acts: physiological acts like sensation, digestion, breathing, blinking or growth. They are contained in this human "blueprint" and occur "automatically," as it were, independent of a direct command from the will.

However, not all acts are automatic. Man performs free acts in his capacity as a rational being endowed with intellect and will. As such, he has the power to do or not do these actions as he so chooses.

Nevertheless, these acts are also subject to rules of behavior established by the Creator. This supreme ordering of human conduct, this *moral* "blueprint" inscribed by the Creator in man's very nature, is called "natural law."

This natural law reflects in man the eternal law, which is simply the Divine Wisdom ruling the universe and establishing a supreme order and governance of all things, visible and invisible, living and inanimate.

As its name indicates, natural law flows from human nature. It is that law which man can know with the light of reason without the aid of Divine Revelation, since God inscribed it in the depths of all hearts as Saint Paul teaches.[2] Since it is inscribed on the hearts of all men, it is the same for everyone, everywhere and throughout time. Thus, natural law is **universal**. It is also **immutable**; time does not affect it. Moreover, there is **no dispensation** from natural law. All men must observe it. Lastly, it is **perceptible** and **knowable** by all men who have reached the age of reason.[3]

Man's conscience assures him of the existence of this law when it declares certain actions good and others bad.[4] Its existence is further attested to by the common witness of all peoples, for they are unanimous in making the distinction between good and evil.

---

2. "For when the Gentiles who do not have the law by nature observe the prescriptions of the law, they are a law for themselves even though they do not have the law. They show that the demands of the law are written in their hearts, while their conscience also bears witness and their conflicting thoughts accuse or even defend them" (Rom. 2:14-15).

3. Cf. Msgr. Guiseppe Graneris, s.v. "Natural Law," *Dictionary of Moral Theology*, p. 697.

4. Coppens, p. 26.

Though they may err at times in their application, the most primitive peoples believe in the existence of universal principles such as, "We must love the supreme good," "Do good and avoid evil," "Do unto others as you would have them do unto you" and "Live according to right reason."

All other principles stem from these universal principles: the respect due to one's parents; the prohibition of homicide, theft, adultery, incest, lying and calumny; in sum, all of the Ten Commandments except the third (Keep holy the Sabbath), which is a Divine positive law.

SIN'S METAPHYSICAL DIMENSION

Unlike irrational creatures, man is endowed with intellect and free will and thus is the master of his conduct. He can act or refrain from acting. He can act in one way or another.

Nevertheless, while man is free to act, his liberty to do so is not absolute. He is not morally free to do what right reason tells him is wrong. This is explained well by Fr. Charles Coppens, S.J.:

> Human acts are those of which a man is master, which he has the power of doing or not doing as he pleases. True, we are *physically free* to perform certain acts or to omit them—to do one thing or its contrary, to choose this act rather than some other; but are we also *morally free* in regard to all such acts? Is it right for me on all occasions to do whatever my inclination prompts me to do? My reason plainly answers, No: it is evident even to a child that some actions are good in themselves, *morally good*, and others bad in themselves, *morally bad*. The good acts our reason com-

mends and approves; these we call *right*. Evil acts, on
the contrary, our reason disapproves and blames; these
we call *wrong*.[5]

When man strays from the divine blueprint inscribed in his
nature, he deviates from the right path and fails to attain the
end for which his nature was created. This failure constitutes
sin in its first, most elementary meaning. The words *hamartia*
in Greek and *peccatum* in Latin (sin in English) mean "fail."
Thus, to sin means to have failed, to miss the target like an
arrow shot by a bad archer. When one misses the target, one
sins. He who does not act according to natural law will never
attain his true end.

More than the moral aspect of sin, there is its profound
metaphysical dimension. More than just disobeying a positive
law, it is a deviation from the end assigned to human nature by
the Creator.

When man abandons the Creator's plan consciously and
maliciously, and not out of human frailty, his actions constitute
a supreme revolt against the wise and marvelous order God
established in the universe.

---

5.   Ibid. (Emphasis in the original.)

"If God didn't exist, everything would be possible"—*Dostoevsky*

If God did not exist, if His ordering Wisdom, the Eternal Law, was not the ultimate reference for human acts, there would be no fixed standard of morals, and man could act as he well pleased.

However, the general order God established in the universe is inscribed in man's heart. This first beacon of truth, known by all men everywhere and throughout time, is natural law. Its most fundamental tenet beckons to man constantly: "Do good and avoid evil."

Thus, although the Gentiles did not receive the law of Moses, Saint Paul teaches that it was nevertheless possible for them to live by its moral precepts, since they knew "by nature those things that are of the law," having "the law written in their hearts." Consequently, "their conscience bears witness to them" (Romans 2:14-15).

Those who would smother the voice of conscience and reject natural law must first deny God's existence. Only then can they justify to themselves the building of their own universe and the making of their own rules.

This is why the atheistic existentialist philosopher, Jean-Paul Sartre, took Dostoevsky's quote as the starting point of his own anarchic philosophy:

> Dostoevsky said, "If God didn't exist, everything would be possible." That is the very starting point of existentialism. Indeed, everything is permissible if God does not exist, and as a result man is forlorn, because neither

within him nor without does he find anything to
cling to.[6]

Indeed, if God did not exist, everything would be possible.
There would be no objective moral standard based on eternal and unchanging truths. Without the order God established in the universe, or if it were unintelligible, man
would be like flotsam on a sea of nonsense. He would be
adrift in complete relativism. His actions, bereft of rationality, would not have a moral dimension.

Contrary to Sartre's anarchic sentiments, man would not
be truly free. He would fall victim to every whim and
fantasy. He would be a slave, locked into the tyrannical
shackles of unbridled passion.

6. "Quotations: Jean-Paul Sartre," www.dividingline.com/private/Philosophy/
    TopPage/Sartre2_Quote.shtml.

CHAPTER 17
The Voice of the Apostles

The Church can say of Herself with Saint Paul: "In receiving the word of God from hearing us, you received not a human word but, as it truly is, the word of God."[1]

Indeed, it is the Church's role to proclaim and safeguard Our Lord's Divine teaching.[2] Thus the Church condemns all forms of immorality, especially those opposed to the natural order as is homosexuality.

This condemnation can be traced to the very beginning of the Church. It continues with the early Church Fathers and ecclesiastical writers, and then the Popes, saints and councils up to the present. Indeed, it could be no different, since "the word of the Lord remains forever."[3] Thus, Saint Peter affirms that the unnatural sins of Sodom and Gomorrah moved God to reduce their cities to ashes.[4] As mentioned earlier, Saint Jude's Epistle also condemns homosexuality.[5]

This was the consistent teaching of all the Apostles.[6]

SAINT PAUL: DEFINING THE POSITION OF THE APOSTLES

Saint Paul, the Apostle to the Gentiles, had a profound

---

1. 1 Thess. 2:13.
2. "Whoever loves Me will keep My word, and My Father will love him, and We will come to him and make Our dwelling with him" (John 14:23). Concerning why Our Lord allows His Church to go through crises and how the existence of bad shepherds (hirelings) and sin in general in the Catholic Church do not taint Her sanctity, see our 2002 book, *I Have Weathered Other Storms*, particularly the Introduction.
3. 1 Peter 1:25.
4. 2 Peter 2:6.
5. Jude 1:7. See Chapter 15.
6. *The Didache* or *The Doctrine of the Apostles* is a small treatise on dogma and morals that summarizes the doctrine of the Apostles. It was written in the second century. In the second chapter, it reads: "And the second commandment of the Teaching...you shall not commit pederasty" (*Didache*, English translation by Roberts-Donaldson, www.earlychristianwritings.com/text/didache-roberts.html).

knowledge of the Greco-Roman world, whose culture spread throughout the Mediterranean basin and Asia Minor. In his epistles, he contrasted Christian marriage, virginity and continence for the love of God with the pagan world's immorality, adultery, prostitution, incest and homosexuality, all of which he condemned.[7] He admonished Christian converts continuously that the impure do not enter the Kingdom of Heaven.[8] The pure, on the contrary, enjoy "citizenship in heaven."[9]

AS A PUNISHMENT, GOD DELIVERS
SINNERS TO THEIR PASSIONS

In his Epistle to the Romans, Saint Paul explains in detail why idolatrous peoples, such as the Romans, fell headlong into unnatural vice.[10] He traces the cause to substituting the worship of the true God with a man-made imitation: idols.

By way of proving that the Gentiles had the means to know God and His law, Saint Paul explains how all of creation reflects God and one can know the Author by contemplating His works.

> The wrath of God is indeed being revealed from heaven against every impiety and wickedness of those who suppress the truth by their wickedness. For what can be known about God is evident to them, because God made it evident to them. Ever since the creation of the world, His invisible attributes of eternal power and divinity have been able to be understood and perceived in what He has made. As a result, they have no excuse; for although they knew God they did not

---

7. *Continence for the love of God*: Eph. 5:21-33; 1 Cor. 7. *Adultery*: Rom. 13:9; Heb. 13:4. *Prostitution*: 1 Cor. 6:13-20; 10:8; 2 Cor. 12:21: Col. 3:5. *Incest*: 1 Cor. 5:1-5. *Homosexuality*: 1 Cor. 6:9-10; Rom. 1:18-32; 1 Tim. 1:10.
8. Eph. 5:5; 1 Cor. 6:9-10; 1 Cor. 15:50; Gal. 5:19-21; Col. 3:5-6.
9. Phil. 3:19-20.
10. Rom. 1:18-32.

accord Him glory as God or give Him thanks.[11]

Thus, the Apostle rebukes the Romans for despising this truth known as such. He concludes that their capital sin was impiety, since they denied God the twofold tributes owed to Him: glorification for being who He is and thanksgiving for the benefits received from Him. This failure to recognize God started a process which corrupted the will, confounded the intellect and finally led to an abyss of disgrace.

Saint Paul describes this process of degradation: By letting themselves be carried away by vanity, they ended up falling into idolatry. God's punishment was to abandon them to their own passions, which led them to vice against nature:

> Instead, they became vain in their reasoning, and their senseless minds were darkened. While claiming to be wise, they became fools and exchanged the glory of the immortal God for the likeness of an image of mortal man or of birds or of four-legged animals or of snakes. Therefore, God handed them over to impurity through the lusts of their hearts for the mutual degradation of their bodies.[12]

The Apostle is not ambiguous. He specifically defines this mutual degradation as the practice of homosexuality and stresses its unnatural character:

> Their females exchanged natural relations for unnatural, and the males likewise gave up natural relations with females and burned with lust for one another. Males did shameful things with males and

---

11. Rom. 1:18-21.
12. Rom. 1:21-24.

thus received in their own persons the due penalty for
their perversity.[13]

The process of decadence had terrible effects. Saint Paul
concludes that, when God abandoned the Romans to this
nefarious vice,[14] it brought dire consequences upon them:

> They are filled with every form of wickedness,
> evil, greed, and malice; full of envy, murder, rivalry,
> treachery, and spite. They are gossips and scandal-
> mongers and they hate God. They are insolent,
> haughty, boastful, ingenious in their wickedness, and
> rebellious toward their parents. They are senseless,
> faithless, heartless, ruthless.[15]

In the final stage of the process, the sinner not only becomes
attached to the sin but tries to justify it, applauding those who
have fallen or recruiting others: "they not only do them but
give approval to those who practice them."[16]

PRIDE IS THE SOURCE OF IMPURITY

Cornelius a Lapide, commenting on this passage of Saint
Paul, emphasizes the role of pride as the origin of all impurity:

---

13. Rom. 1:26-27.
14. "In this complex act of divine justice three elements can be distinguished: per-
mission, without which no evil is possible; partial abandonment—that is to say,
a withdrawal of chosen graces, which leaves intact the free will with moral
responsibility, but increases the probability of falling into sin by reason of
diminished aid; finally, a judgment, by which God withdraws his graces, as a
punishment for men's malice, ingratitude, and obstinacy. Thus the first sin
becomes the cause (not necessary but incidental) of the second; and the second
is the real, though indirect punishment of the first" (Fernand Prat, S.J., *The
Theology of Saint Paul* [Westminster, Md.: The Newman Bookshop, 1952], Vol.
1, p. 201).
15. Rom. 1:25, 28-31.
16. Rom. 1:32. Cf. Gal. 5:19-21.

Impurity is a punishment for pride, just as humility is the reward for chastity. This is the just order established by God, and if man submits his mind to God, so also his body will be submitted to God. On the contrary, when man rebels against God, his body also rebels against him, as St. Gregory (lib. XXVI, *Morals*, xii) beautifully teaches….[T]hrough humility the purity of chastity is guaranteed. Indeed, if one submits piously to God, one's flesh will not rise illicitly against the spirit. That is why Adam, the first to disobey, covered himself as soon as he had committed the sin of pride.[17]

---

17. Cornelius a Lapide, *Commentaria in Scripturam Sacram*, (Paris: Vivès, 1863), Vol. 18, p. 54. For a more extensive discussion of the role of pride and apostasy from God as sources of impurity, see Chapter 5 of our book *I Have Weathered Other Storms*.

CHAPTER 18
Church Fathers and Doctors Condemn Homosexuality

The Church Fathers are witnesses of divine Tradition.[1] They, too, condemned homosexuality in their writings. Since their condemnations and those made by Ecclesiastical Writers[2] are so numerous, only a few samples are given below. Also included are some quotes from Doctors of the Church.[3]

SAINT JUSTIN THE MARTYR (100-165)

Saint Justin, martyr and Christian apologist, was born in Flavia Neapolis and converted to Christianity about 130. He taught and defended the Christian religion in Asia Minor and Rome, where he suffered martyrdom.

In his *First Apology*, addressed to the Emperor Titus, Saint Justin explains the Christian mysteries and the rationality of Catholic doctrine. He also points out paganism's absurdity and the immorality of the Greeks and Romans:

But as for us, we have been taught that to expose

---

1. *Fathers of the Church*: Christian writers notable for their doctrine, holiness and antiquity. The Patristic Era spans from the 1st to the 8th centuries. "The morally unanimous concord of the Fathers in matters of faith or morals is an irrefragable testimony of divine Tradition" (s.v. "Fathers of the Church," in Pietro Parente, Antonio Piolanti, and Salvatore Garofalo, *Dictionary of Dogmatic Theology* [Milwaukee: The Bruce Publishing Company, 1952], p. 103).

2. *Ecclesiastical Writers*: Christian authors of the early Church notable for their erudition but lacking the note of sanctity. Some of them have grave errors in parts of their works or even apostatized from the Faith. However, their orthodox writings are normally quoted by the Popes and theologians, as is the case of Tertullian, Origin, Clement of Alexandria and others.

3. *Doctor of the Church*: An official title bestowed by the Church on saints who are recognized as having been outstanding in sanctity and in their orthodoxy of doctrine. This title must be explicitly granted by the Pope. Some Doctors of the Church from the first centuries are also Fathers, like St. Jerome. Others, such as St. Thomas Aquinas or St. Alphonsus Liguori, lived after the Patristic Era. Currently there are 33 Doctors of the Church. The most recent Doctor is Saint Thérèse of the Child Jesus. She was made Doctor of the Church by Pope John Paul II in 1997.

newly-born children is the part of wicked men; and this we have been taught lest we should do any one an injury, and lest we should sin against God, first, because we see that almost all so exposed (not only the girls, but also the males) are brought up to prostitution. And as the ancients are said to have reared herds of oxen, or goats, or sheep, or grazing horses, so now we see you rear children only for this shameful use; and for this pollution a multitude of females and hermaphrodites, and those who commit unmentionable iniquities, are found in every nation. And you receive the hire of these, and duty and taxes from them, whom you ought to exterminate from your realm. And any one who uses such persons, besides the godless and infamous and impure intercourse, may possibly be having intercourse with his own child, or relative, or brother. And there are some who prostitute even their own children and wives, and some are openly mutilated for the purpose of sodomy.[4]

SAINT IRENAEUS OF LYONS (130-202)

Saint Irenaeus was born in Smyrna, in Asia Minor, where he met Bishop Saint Polycarp, a disciple of the Apostle Saint John. Leaving Asia Minor for Rome, Saint Irenaeus joined the school of Saint Justin the Martyr before becoming Bishop of Lyons in Southern Gaul. Saint Irenaeus' best-known writings are *Against Heresies and Proof of the Apostolic Preaching*, in which he refuted Gnosticism.

Saint Irenaeus condemns the doctrines of Marcion and other Gnostics who held that those described as evil in the Old Testament were actually saved, while Abel, Noah and all the just of the Old Testament were damned. In condemning

---

4.   www.newadvent.org/fathers/0126.htm.

Marcion's false teaching, Saint Irenaeus reiterates the Church's condemnation of homosexuality:

> In addition to this blasphemy against God Himself, he [Marcion] advanced this also, truly speaking as with the mouth of the devil, and saying all things in direct opposition to the truth—that Cain, and those like him, and the Sodomites, and the Egyptians, and others like them, and, in fine, all the nations who walked in all sorts of abomination were saved by the Lord.[5]

ATHENAGORAS OF ATHENS (2ND CENTURY)

Athenagoras of Athens was a philosopher who converted to Christianity in the second century. Athenagoras wrote his *Plea for Christians* to the Emperor Marcus Aurelius around 177.

He defended Christians, whom the pagans, misinterpreting Catholic worship, had accused of immorality. He then shows that the pagans, who were totally immoral, did not even refrain from sins against nature:

> But though such is our character (Oh! why should I speak of things unfit to be uttered?), the things said of us are an example of the proverb, "The harlot reproves the chaste." For those who have set up a market for fornication and established infamous resorts for the young for every kind of vile pleasure—who do not abstain even from males, males with males committing shocking abominations, outraging all the noblest and comeliest bodies in all sorts of ways, so dishonoring the fair workmanship of God.[6]

---

5. *Adversus haereses*, Book I, Chap. 27, no. 3, www.newadvent.org/fathers/0103127.htm.
6. Fr. B. P. Pratten, trans., *A Plea For The Christians*, Chap. 34, www.newadvent.org/fathers/0205.htm.

TERTULLIAN (160-225)

Tertullian was a great genius and apologist of the early Church. Unfortunately, after an initial period of fervor, he succumbed to resentment and pride, left the Church and adhered to the Montanist heresy. Because of works written while still in the Church, he is considered an Ecclesiastical Writer and, as such, is commonly quoted by Popes and theologians.

His treatise *On Modesty* is an apology of Christian chastity. He clearly shows the horror the Church has for sins against nature. After condemning adultery, he exclaims:

> But all the other frenzies of passions—impious both toward the bodies and toward the sexes— beyond the laws of nature, we banish not only from the threshold, but from all shelter of the Church, because they are not sins, but monstrosities.[7]

EUSEBIUS OF CÆSAREA (260-341)

Eusebius Pamphili, Bishop of Cæsarea in Palestine and the "Father of Church History," writes in his book, *Demonstratio Evangelica*: "[God in the Law given to Moses] having forbidden all unlawful marriage, and all unseemly practice, and the union of women with women and men with men."[8]

SAINT JEROME (340-420)

Saint Jerome is both Father and Doctor of the Church. He was also a notable exegete and great polemicist. In his book *Against Jovinianus*, he explains how a sodomite needs repentance and penance to be saved: "And Sodom and

---

7. Fr. S. Thelwall, trans., *On Modesty*, Chap. 4, www.ccel.org/fathers2/ANF-04/anf04-19.htm.
8. W. J. Ferrar, trans., *Demonstratio Evangelica*, Book 4, Chap. 10, www.early-christianwritings.com/fathers/eusebius_de_06_book4.htm.

Gomorrah might have appeased it [God's wrath], had they been willing to repent, and through the aid of fasting gain for themselves tears of repentance."[9]

SAINT JOHN CHRYSOSTOM (347-407)

Saint John Chrysostom is considered the greatest of the Greek Fathers and was proclaimed Doctor of the Church. He was given the title "Chrysostom" ("golden-mouthed") because of his great oratorical ability and sermons. He was Archbishop and Patriarch of Constantinople, and his revision of the Greek liturgy is used until today. In his sermons about Saint Paul's Epistle to the Romans, he dwells on the extreme gravity of the sin of homosexuality:

> But if thou scoffest at hearing of hell and believest not that fire, remember Sodom. For we have seen, surely we have seen, even in this present life, a semblance of hell. For since many would utterly disbelieve the things to come after the resurrection, hearing now of an unquenchable fire, God brings them to a right mind by things present. For such is the burning of Sodom, and that conflagration!... Consider how great is that sin, to have forced hell to appear even before its time!... For that rain was unwonted, for the intercourse was contrary to nature, and it deluged the land, since lust had done so with their souls. Wherefore also the rain was the opposite of the customary rain. Now not only did it fail to stir up the womb of the earth to the production of fruits, but made it even useless for the reception of seed. For such was also the intercourse of the men, making a body of this sort more worthless than the very land of Sodom. And what is there more detestable than a man who hath

---

9.   Book 2, no. 15, www.newadvent.org/fathers/30092.htm.

pandered himself, or what more execrable?[10]

SAINT AUGUSTINE (354-430)

The greatest of the Fathers of the West and one of the great Doctors of the Church, Saint Augustine laid the foundations of Catholic theology. In his celebrated *Confessions*, he thus condemns homosexuality:

> Those offences which be contrary to nature are everywhere and at all times to be held in detestation and punished; such were those of the Sodomites, which should all nations commit, they should all be held guilty of the same crime by the divine law, which hath not so made men that they should in that way abuse one another. For even that fellowship which should be between God and us is violated, when that same nature of which He is author is polluted by the perversity of lust.[11]

SAINT GREGORY THE GREAT (540-604)

Pope Saint Gregory I is called "the Great." He is both Father and Doctor of the Church. He introduced Gregorian chant into the Church. Having come across some young Angle slaves being sold at the market in Rome, he bought their freedom, saying: "They are not Angles, but angels." He then organized England's conversion, sending Saint Augustine of Canterbury and many Benedictine monks there.

> Sacred Scripture itself confirms that sulfur evokes the stench of the flesh, as it speaks of the rain of fire

---

10. *Homily IV Romans* 1:26-27, www.ccel.org/fathers/NPNF111/Chrysostom/Romans/Rom-Hom04.html.
11. Book III, Chap. 8, no. 15, www.newadvent.org/fathers/110103.htm.

and sulfur poured upon Sodom by the Lord. He had decided to punish Sodom for the crimes of the flesh, and the very type of punishment he chose emphasized the shame of that crime. For sulfur stinks, and fire burns. So it was just that Sodomites, burning with perverse desires arising from the flesh like stench, should perish by fire and sulfur so that through this just punishment they would realize the evil they had committed, led by a perverse desire.[12]

SAINT PETER DAMIAN (1007-1072)

Doctor of the Church, cardinal and a great reformer of the clergy, Saint Peter Damian wrote his famous *Book of Gomorrah* against the inroads made by homosexuality among the clergy. He describes not only the iniquity of homosexuality, but also its psychological and moral consequences:

Truly, this vice is never to be compared with any other vice because it surpasses the enormity of all vices.... It defiles everything, stains everything, pollutes everything. And as for itself, it permits nothing pure, nothing clean, nothing other than filth....

The miserable flesh burns with the heat of lust; the cold mind trembles with the rancor of suspicion; and in the heart of the miserable man chaos boils like Tartarus [Hell].... In fact, after this most poisonous serpent once sinks its fangs into the unhappy soul, sense is snatched away, memory is borne off, the sharpness of the mind is obscured. It becomes unmindful of God and even forgetful of itself. This plague undermines the foundation of faith, weakens the strength of hope, destroys the bond of charity; it

---

12. *Morales sur Job*, Part III, Vol. I, book 14, no. 23, p. 353. (Our translation.)

takes away justice, subverts fortitude, banishes temperance, blunts the keenness of prudence.

And what more should I say since it expels the whole host of the virtues from the chamber of the human heart and introduces every barbarous vice as if the bolts of the doors were pulled out.[13]

SAINT THOMAS AQUINAS (1225-1274)

Commenting upon Saint Paul's Epistle to the Romans (1:26-27), Saint Thomas Aquinas, the Angelic Doctor, explains why the sin of homosexuality is so grave:

Given the sin of impiety through which they [the Romans] sinned against the divine nature [by idolatry], the punishment that led them to sin against their own nature followed.... I say, therefore, that since they changed into lies [by idolatry] the truth about God, He brought them to ignominious passions, that is, to sins against nature; not that God led them to evil, but only that he abandoned them to evil....

If all the sins of the flesh are worthy of condemnation because by them man allows himself to be dominated by that which he has of the animal nature, much more deserving of condemnation are the sins against nature by which man degrades his own animal nature....

Man can sin against nature in two ways. First, when he sins against his specific rational nature, acting contrary to reason. In this sense, we can say that every sin is a sin against man's nature, because it is against man's right reason....

13. St. Peter Damian, *Book of Gomorrah*, Pierre J. Payer, trans., (Waterloo, Ont.: Wilfrid Laurier University Press, 1982), pp. 63-64.

Secondly, man sins against nature when he goes against his generic nature, that is to say, his animal nature. Now, it is evident that, in accord with natural order, the union of the sexes among animals is ordered towards conception. From this it follows that every sexual intercourse that cannot lead to conception is opposed to man's animal nature.[14]

SAINT CATHERINE OF SIENA (1347-1380)

Saint Catherine, a great mystic and Doctor of the Church, lived in troubled times. The Papacy was in exile at Avignon, France. She was instrumental in bringing the Popes back to Rome. Her famous *Dialogues* are written as if dictated by God Himself:

But they act in a contrary way, for they come full of impurity to this mystery, and not only of that impurity to which, through the fragility of your weak nature, you are all naturally inclined (although reason, when free will permits, can quiet the rebellion of nature), but these wretches not only do not bridle this fragility, but do worse, committing that accursed sin against nature, and as blind and fools, with the light of their intellect darkened, they do not know the stench and misery in which they are. It is not only that this sin stinks before me, who am the Supreme and Eternal Truth, it does indeed displease me so much and I hold it in such abomination that for it alone I buried five cities by a divine judgment, my divine justice being no longer able to endure it. This sin not only displeases me as I have said, but also the

---

14. St. Thomas Aquinas, *Super Epistolam B. Pauli ad Romanos*, Cap. 1, Lec. 8, www.unav.es/filosofia/alarcon/amicis/cro016.html. (Our translation.)

devils whom these wretches have made their masters. Not that the evil displeases them because they like anything good, but because their nature was originally angelic, and their angelic nature causes them to loathe the sight of the actual commission of this enormous sin.[15]

SAINT BERNARDINE OF SIENA (1380-1444)

Saint Bernardine of Siena was a famous preacher, celebrated for his doctrine and holiness. Regarding homosexuality, he stated:

> No sin in the world grips the soul as the accursed sodomy; this sin has always been detested by all those who live according to God.... Deviant passion is close to madness; this vice disturbs the intellect, destroys elevation and generosity of soul, brings the mind down from great thoughts to the lowliest, makes the person slothful, irascible, obstinate and obdurate, servile and soft and incapable of anything; further-more, agitated by an insatiable craving for pleasure, the person follows not reason but frenzy.... They become blind and, when their thoughts should soar to high and great things, they are broken down and reduced to vile and useless and putrid things, which could never make them happy.... Just as people participate in the glory of God in different degrees, so also in hell some suffer more than others. He who lived with this vice of sodomy suffers more than another, for this is the greatest sin.[16]

---

15. St. Catherine of Siena, *The Dialogue of the Seraphic Virgin* (London: Burns, Oates and Washbourne, Ltd., 1925), p. 255.
16. St. Bernardine of Siena, *Sermon XXXIX* in *Prediche volgari*, pp. 896-897, 915.

SAINT PETER CANISIUS (1521-1597)

Saint Peter Canisius, Jesuit and Doctor of the Church, is responsible for helping one third of Germany abandon Lutheranism and return to the Church. To Scripture's condemnation of homosexuality, he added his own:

> As the Sacred Scripture says, the Sodomites were wicked and exceedingly sinful. Saint Peter and Saint Paul condemn this nefarious and depraved sin. In fact, the Scripture denounces this enormous indecency thus: "The scandal of Sodomites and Gomorrhans has multiplied and their sins have become grave beyond measure." So the angels said to just Lot, who totally abhorred the depravity of the Sodomites: "Let us leave this city... ." Holy Scripture does not fail to mention the causes that led the Sodomites, and can also lead others, to this most grievous sin. In fact, in Ezechiel we read: "Behold this was the iniquity of Sodom: pride, fullness of bread, and abundance, and the idleness of her, and of her daughters: and they did not put forth their hand to the needy, and the poor. And they were lifted up, and committed abominations before me; and I took them away as thou hast seen" (Ezech. 16:49-50). Those unashamed of violating divine and natural law are slaves of this never sufficiently execrated depravity.[17]

---

17. St. Peter Canisius, *Summa Doctrina Christianae*, III a/b, p. 455.

CHAPTER 19
Ecclesiastical Discipline:
Translating Words into Action

The Church's condemnation of homosexuality is also reflected in ecclesiastical discipline. Thus, from the earliest times, disciplinary measures against homosexuality were adopted in councils and synods, penitential manuals for confessors, internal regulations of religious orders, papal decretals and, more recently, the Code of Canon Law. A few examples of this ocean of disciplinary measures adopted over 2,000 years are provided in this chapter.

COUNCILS AND SYNODS

Conciliar and synodal condemnations of homosexuality for which records exist date to the Council of Elvira in Spain (canon 71), held in 306. Of all ecclesiastical assemblies,[1] the Third Lateran Ecumenical Council held in 1179 gave the most decisive contribution to Canon Law and the general discipline of the Church regarding homosexuality. Canon 11 of this council reads:

> Let all who are found guilty of that unnatural vice
> for which the wrath of God came down upon the sons
> of disobedience and destroyed the five cities with fire,
> if they are clerics be expelled from the clergy or
> confined in monasteries to do penance; if they are laymen

---

1. Other councils and synods that condemn homosexuality, in chronological order, include: 314—Council of Ancyra in Galatia (canons 16-17); 567—The Second Council of Tours, France (canon 14); 693—The Sixteenth Council of Toledo, Spain (canon 3); 829—The Council of Paris (canons 34 and 69); 909—Council of Trosly (canon 15); 1049—Council of Rheims; 1102—The Council of London (canons 28 and 29); 1120—The Council of Nablus (canons 8-11); 1212—Synod of Paris; 1214—Synod of Rouen; 1215—The Fourth Lateran Ecumenical Council (canon 14); 1216-1219—Synod of Angers; 1246—Synod of Beziers. Cf. Pierre J. Payer, Introduction to St. Peter Damian, *Book of Gomorrah*.

they are to incur excommunication and be completely separated from the society of the faithful.[2]

The Fifth Lateran Ecumenical Council (1512-1517) established that any member of the clergy caught practicing homosexuality be released from his clerical orders or constrained to do penance in a monastery.[3]

DECRETALS AND OTHER PONTIFICAL DECISIONS

Decretals were papal decisions on matters of discipline issued as papal determinations in Church appeals or when papal guidance was solicited. Collections of decretals compiled in the Middle Ages were important in the development of Canon Law.

The most famous collection is known as *The Decretum of Gratian*. It was compiled around 1148 by Gratian, a monk from Bologna, Italy. This *Decretum* also mentions homosexuality.

Another decretal is a letter from Pope Innocent III issued in 1203 on the practice of homosexuality in Macon, France.[4]

In 1233, Pope Gregory IX issued the Bull "Vox in Rama," condemning the activities of Conrad of Marburg, a heretical leader who indulged in bisexual orgies.[5] In the following year, the same Pope issued the Bull "Liber Extra," reiterating the canon adopted in the Third Lateran Council in 1179.[6]

On April 1, 1566, Pope Saint Pius V issued the Bull "Cum Primum," which reads:

2. Third Lateran Ecumenical Council, Canon 11, www.ewtn/library/COUN-CILS/LATERAN3.HTM.
3. Cf. Roberto de Mattei, ed., *Eglise et Homosexualite* (Paris: Pierre Tequi, 1995), p. 19.
4. In J.P. Migne, ed., *Patrologia Latina*, 215:189, www.geocities.com/pharsea/ScrapingTheBarrel.html.
5. Cf. www.geocities.com/pharsea/ScrapingTheBarrel.html .
6. Ibid.

Having set our sights on removing everything that can somehow offend the divine majesty, We resolved to punish above all, and without leniency, those things which, on the authority of Sacred Scripture or with most grave examples, are known to displease God and provoke his ire more than any others: namely, neglect of divine worship, ruinous simony, the crime of blasphemy, and the execrable libidinous vice against nature; for these faults people and nations are justly scourged by God with catastrophes, wars, famine and pestilence....

If anyone commits the nefarious crime against nature, which caused God's wrath to fall upon the sons of iniquity, he will be delivered to the secular arm for punishment, and, if a cleric, he will be subject to analogous penalty after being stripped of his office.[7]

On August 30, 1568, Pope Saint Pius V issued a second Bull "Horrendum illud scelus," which reads:

That horrendous crime, for which the corrupt and obscene cities [of Sodom and Gomorrah] were burned by divine condemnation, fills us with most bitter pain and strongly prods us to repress such crime with the greatest possible zeal. With every reason the Fifth Lateran Council [1512-1517] establishes that any member of the clergy caught in that vice against nature, for which the divine wrath fell upon the sons of iniquity, be released from his clerical orders or constrained to do penance in a monastery (c. 4, X, V, 31). So that the contagion of such a great scourge will

---

7. St. Pius V, Bull "Cum Primum," in *Bullarium Romanum*, Vol. 4, Chap. 2, pp. 284-286. (Our translation.)

not grow with greater audacity by profiting from impunity, which is the greatest incentive to sin, and in order to chastise more severely the clerics guilty of this nefarious crime who are not terrified with the death of the soul, We have decided that they be chastened by the secular authority, which enforces civil law.

Therefore, wishing to pursue with greater vigor what We had decreed since the beginning of Our Pontificate (Bull "Cum Primum"), We establish that any priest or member of the clergy, whether secular or regular, of any rank or dignity, who commits such a horrific crime, by virtue of the present law be deprived of any clerical privilege, post, dignity and ecclesiastical benefit, and, once degraded by the ecclesiastical Judge, be consigned to the civil authority so he may be dealt the same punishment the law reserves for lay people who have slid into this abyss.[8]

In his 1910 Catechism, Pope Saint Pius X says that sodomy ranks second in gravity to voluntary homicide, among the sins that "cry out to God for vengeance." "These sins," the Catechism explains, "are said to cry out to God because the Holy Spirit says so and because their iniquity is so grave and manifest that it provokes God to punish with more severe chastisements."[9]

THE 1917 CODE OF CANON LAW

Pope Saint Pius X started the project of codifying Church law but did not live to see it completed. His successor, Pope Benedict XV, promulgated the Code of Canon Law in 1917. It

---

8.   St. Pius V, Bull "Horrendum illud scelus," in *Bullarium Romanum*, Vol. 4, Chap. 3, p. 33. (Our translation.)
9.   St. Pius X, *Catechism of St. Pius X*, www.ewtn.com/library/CATECHISM/PIUSXCAT.HTM.

incorporated all internal disciplinary norms accumulated by the Church over nineteen centuries.

Lay persons who committed the legal offense or delict of sodomy were punished ipso facto, with the penalty of infamy,[10] and with other sanctions at the prudent discretion of the local bishop. Canon 2357, § 1:

> Lay persons who have been legally found guilty of a crime of sexual immorality committed with a minor under sixteen years of age, or rape, sodomy, incest, pandering, are ipso facto infamous, besides being subject to other penalties which the Ordinary may deem proper to inflict.

Canon 2358 provided that clerics in minor orders (those not yet subdeacons or higher) could be punished "even by the dismissal from the clerical state."

As for clerics in major orders (deacon, priest and bishop) the 1917 Code provided that:

> If they have committed a crime against the sixth commandment with a minor under sixteen years of age, or have committed adultery, rape, bestiality, sodomy, pandering, or incest with any person related to them by consanguinity or affinity in the first degree, they shall be suspended, declared infamous, deprived of any office, benefice, dignity, or position they may have, and, in more serious cases, shall be deposed.[11]

---

10. *Infamy*: "A stigma attaching in canon law to the character of a person. It is of two kinds: *infamia facti* (of fact) or loss of good name by reason of crime or evil conduct; and *infamia juris* (of law) or stigma attached by common law to certain persons as a vindicative penalty" (Donald Attwater, s.v. "Infamy," in *A Catholic Dictionary* [New York: The MacMillan Company, 1953], p. 254).

11. T. Lincoln Bouscaren, S.J., and Adam C. Ellis, S.J., *Canon Law: A Text and Commentary* (Milwaukee: The Bruce Publishing Co., 1953), pp. 931-932.

Being *infamous*, lay persons and clerics who committed the delict of sodomy were automatically relegated to the state of irregularity: "An irregularity may be defined as a perpetual impediment established by ecclesiastical law forbidding primarily the reception of orders and secondarily the exercise of orders already received."[12]

THE 1983 CODE OF CANON LAW

In 1983, Pope John Paul II promulgated a revised Code of Canon Law. This new Code maintains the sanction for clergymen who sin against chastity, even though it fails to specify, with the exception of concubinage, the various "external sins against the sixth commandment." The pertinent section is Canon 1395, which reads as follows:

> §1. Outside the case mentioned in can. 1394, a cleric who lives in concubinage or a cleric who remains in another external sin against the sixth commandment of the Decalogue which produces scandal is to be punished with suspension; and, if such a cleric persists in such an offense after having been admonished, other penalties can be added gradually including dismissal from the clerical state.
>
> §2. If a cleric has otherwise committed an offense against the sixth commandment of the Decalogue with force or threats or publicly or with a minor below the age of sixteen, the cleric is to be punished with just penalties, including the dismissal from the clerical state if the case warrants it.[13]

---

12. Ibid., p. 913.
13. James A. Coriden, Thomas J. Green and Donald E. Heinstchel, eds., *The Code of Canon Law: A Text and Commentary* (New York: Paulist Press, 1985), p. 929.

Commentary provided by canonist Thomas J. Green says the mention of concubinage in the first paragraph "also encompasses other *habitual* sexual offenses by a cleric that involve scandal yet not the exclusivity of the concubinary relationship." Commenting on the second paragraph, he says: "Paragraph two deals with certain *non-habitual* clerical sexual offenses, which are especially serious if they are perpetrated publicly, or with force or threats, or with a person of either sex under sixteen years of age."[14]

VATICAN DOCUMENT ON THE SELECTION AND TRAINING OF CANDIDATES FOR THE PRIESTHOOD

On February 2, 1961, the Sacred Congregation for Religious promulgated its *Instruction Religiosorum Institutio on Careful Selection and Training of Candidates for the States of Perfection and Sacred Orders*. This Vatican directive was sent directly to the superiors of religious orders and congregations. The document states:

> If a student in a minor seminary has sinned gravely against the sixth commandment with a person of the same or the other sex, or has been the occasion of grave scandal in the matter of chastity, he is to be dismissed immediately as stipulated in canon 1371....
>
> If a novice or a professed religious who has not yet made perpetual vows should be guilty of the same offense, he is to be sent away from the community or, should the circumstances so demand, he is to be dismissed with due observance of canon 647, § 2, n. 1.
>
> If a perpetually professed religious is found guilty of any such sin, he is to be perpetually excluded from tonsure and the reception of any further Order....

---

14. Ibid.

Lastly, should he be a subdeacon or deacon, then, without prejudice to the above-mentioned directives and if the case should so demand, the superiors should take up with the Holy See the question of his reduction to the lay state.

For these reasons, clerics who in their diocese or religious who in another community have sinned gravely against chastity with another person are not to be admitted with a view to the priesthood....

Advancement to religious vows and ordination should be barred to those who are afflicted with evil tendencies to homosexuality or pederasty, since for them the common life and the priestly ministry would constitute serious dangers.[15]

As can be seen, the Catholic Church has always condemned homosexuality in both Her moral doctrine and in Her internal discipline.

---

15. This document was not published in the *Acta Apostolicae Sedis*. It was published, however, in its entirety in English in the *Canon Law Digest* (Milwaukee: The Bruce Publishing Co., 1963), Vol. 5, pp. 452-486. It can be found on many web sites, for instance, www.helpthebishops.com/THE%20CANON%20LAW%20DIGEST.htm.

CHAPTER 20
Recent Church Condemnations
of Homosexuality

Certain modern theologians and writers have created a climate of confusion, claiming that the Church changed her official teaching on homosexuality. However, such claims are completely false. In fact, as the controversy has grown, the Holy See has published a series of statements reaffirming the Church's position. There can be no doubt that the Church's condemnation stands unchanged.

PERSONA HUMANA—
A DECLARATION ON SEXUAL ETHICS

On December 29, 1975, amid the abandonment of Christian morality caused by the sexual revolution, the Sacred Congregation for the Doctrine of the Faith published the document *Persona Humana—Declaration on Certain Questions Concerning Sexual Ethics*.[1] It denounces the prevalent moral subjectivism, which many theologians were defending based on a misguided pastoral approach.

Persona Humana describes the sexual revolution's influence over all of society, particularly through the media, and reminds Catholics that morals depend not on human whims or changing cultures, but on natural law.

The declaration recalls the categorical doctrine of the Church and of natural ethics that every sexual act outside marriage is sinful. It thus condemns pre-marital sex, cohabitation, masturbation and homosexuality.[2] The document condemns the conclusion that a stable homosexual relationship analogous to marriage could be justified:

---

1. It is available at www.vatican.va/roman_curia/congregations/cfaith/coduments/ rc_con_cfaith?doc?19751229_persona-humana_en.html. Hereafter *Persona Humana*. (Original footnotes are omitted.)
2. *Persona Humana*, VII, IX.

No pastoral method can be employed which would give moral justification to these acts on the grounds that they would be consonant with the condition of such people. For according to the objective moral order, homosexual relations are acts which lack an essential and indispensable finality.[3]

LETTER ON THE PASTORAL
CARE OF HOMOSEXUAL PERSONS

On October 1, 1986, the Sacred Congregation for the Doctrine of the Faith published a new document titled *Letter to the Bishops of the Catholic Church on the Pastoral Care of Homosexual Persons.*[4]

The *Letter* recalls the distinction between homosexual tendencies and homosexual practices:

Although the particular inclination of the homosexual person is not a sin, it is a more or less strong tendency ordered toward an intrinsic moral evil; and thus the inclination itself must be seen as an objective disorder.[5]

The *Letter* also condemns the errors of biblical exegetes that favored homosexuality, saying there is not even a shadow of doubt about scriptures' moral condemnation of homosexuality.[6]

After recalling the doctrine that sexual intercourse is legitimate only in matrimony, the *Letter* affirms: "A person engaging in homosexual behavior therefore acts immorally."[7]

---

3. *Persona Humana*, VIII.
4. Congregation for the Doctrine of the Faith, *Letter to the Bishops of the Catholic Church on the Pastoral Care of Homosexual Persons.* Hereafter referred to as *Letter*. It is available at www.vatican.va/roman_curia/congregations/cfaith/documents/rc_con_cfaith_doc_19861001_homosexual-persons_en.html.
5. *Letter*, no. 3.
6. *Letter*, no. 6.
7. *Letter*, no. 7.

While condemning crimes committed against homosexuals, the *Letter* contends that these crimes cannot serve as a pretext to justify homosexuality, let alone create special legislation to protect a condemnable behavior.

The *Letter* says that those afflicted with same-sex attraction will find solutions for their difficult situation in the Cross of Our Lord:

> Fundamentally, they are called to enact the will of God in their life by joining whatever sufferings and difficulties they experience in virtue of their condition to the sacrifice of the Lord's Cross.[8]

ENCYCLICAL *VERITATIS SPLENDOR*

In 1993, Pope John Paul II published his encyclical *Veritatis Splendor* on fundamental issues involving the Church's moral teaching.[9] The encyclical is an important reaffirmation of natural law and the Church's perennial condemnation of homosexuality.

Certain theologians claimed that the documents of the Magisterium, particularly regarding sexual and conjugal morals, were influenced by an understanding of natural law that presented as "moral laws what are in themselves mere biological laws." This "naturalistic understanding of the sexual act," they claimed, is why practices such as "contraception, direct sterilization, autoeroticism, pre-marital sexual relations, homosexual relations and artificial insemination were condemned as morally unacceptable."[10]

---

8. *Letter*, no. 12.
9. John Paul II, Encyclical *Veritatis Splendor*, Aug. 6, 1993, www.vatican.va/holy_father/john_paul_ii/encyclicals/documents/hf_jp-ii_enc_06081993_veritatis-splendor_en.htm.
10. *Veritatis Splendor*, no. 47.

Opposing these errors, the encyclical affirms:

> In teaching the existence of intrinsically evil acts,
> the Church accepts the teaching of Sacred Scripture.
> The Apostle Paul emphatically states, "Do not be
> deceived: neither the immoral, nor idolaters, nor
> adulterers, nor sexual perverts, nor thieves, nor the
> greedy, nor drunkards, nor revilers, nor robbers will
> inherit the Kingdom of God (1 Cor 6:9-10).[11]

CATECHISM OF THE CATHOLIC CHURCH

In 1994, the Vatican published the *Catechism of the
Catholic Church*,[12] which restated the doctrine expressed in
previous documents. The *Catechism* clearly teaches that
homosexuality is contrary to nature and that homosexual acts
are among the "sins gravely contrary to chastity."[13]

Homosexual acts are "intrinsically disordered," "contrary to
the natural law" and "under no circumstances can they be
approved."[14] The homosexual inclination "is objectively disordered," but those affected by it "must be accepted with respect,
compassion, and sensitivity," without "unjust discrimination."
They are called "to fulfill God's will in their lives and, if they
are Christians, to unite to the sacrifice of the Lord's Cross the
difficulties they may encounter from their condition."[15]

---

11. *Veritatis Splendor*, no. 81.
12. The *Catechism of the Catholic Church* was originally published in French and
translated into many languages and published throughout the world. The Latin
Typical Edition, with many corrections, was published in 1997. The current
English version is based on this Typical Edition. We quote from the English version available online at the Vatican web site: www.vatican.va/archive/ccc_css/
archive/catechism/ccc_toc.htm. (Hereafter CCC).
13. CCC, 2396.
14. CCC, 2357.
15. CCC, 2358.

CHAPTER 21
The Vatican's 2003 Condemnation

The homosexual revolution recently scored major judicial and legislative victories in several countries. This led the Holy See to release yet another document recalling Catholic doctrine on sexual morals, condemning homosexuality and calling on Catholics to oppose the legalization of homosexual unions.

Titled *Considerations Regarding Proposals to Give Legal Recognition to Unions Between Homosexual Persons*, the document was published on July 31, 2003, by the Sacred Congregation for the Doctrine of the Faith. It was signed by the Congregation's Prefect, Joseph Cardinal Ratzinger, and Secretary, Archbishop Angelo Amato.

WRITTEN FOR EVERYONE

Although written for everyone, *Considerations* makes special mention of Catholic bishops and politicians, since they can more directly intervene against the homosexual movement's legislative offensive.

For bishops, *Considerations* is designed to "reiterate the essential points on this question and provide arguments drawn from reason" so they can carry out "more specific interventions." These arguments are also useful to Catholic politicians whose public lives must be "consistent with Christian conscience." Finally, *Considerations* is addressed to "all persons committed to promoting and defending the common good of society."[1] It presents arguments based on natural reason.

MARRIAGE EXISTS SOLELY
BETWEEN A MAN AND A WOMAN

Based on the principle that marriage supposes "the complementarity of the sexes," *Considerations* explains that marriage

---

1. *Considerations*, no 1.

"is not just any relationship between human beings. It was established by the Creator with its own nature, essential properties and purpose."

This truth is so evident that "no ideology can erase from the human spirit the certainty that marriage exists solely between a man and a woman."[2]

Considerations continues:

> There are absolutely no grounds for considering homosexual unions to be in any way similar or even remotely analogous to God's plan for marriage and family. Marriage is holy, while **homosexual acts go against the natural moral law**. Homosexual acts "close the sexual act to the gift of life. They do not proceed from a genuine affective and sexual complementarity. Under no circumstances can they be approved."
>
> Sacred Scripture condemns homosexual acts "as a serious depravity.... This judgment of Scripture does not of course permit us to conclude that all those who suffer from this anomaly are personally responsible for it, but it does attest to the fact that homosexual acts are intrinsically disordered." This same moral judgment is found in many Christian writers of the first centuries "and is unanimously accepted by Catholic Tradition."[3]

HOMOSEXUALITY IS A GRAVE SIN AGAINST CHASTITY

After recalling that people with a deviant inclination should be treated with respect and compassion, *Considerations* quotes

2. Ibid., no. 2.
3. Ibid., no. 4.

the *Catechism of the Catholic Church*, which states that such an inclination is "objectively disordered" and that homosexual practices are among the "sins gravely contrary to chastity."[4]

A DUTY TO OFFER CLEAR
AND EMPHATIC OPPOSITION

Considerations points out that the homosexual movement takes advantage of legal tolerance to promote its ideology and place people at risk, particularly youth. It warns "that the approval or legalization of evil is something far different from the toleration of evil."[5] Even where homosexual unions have been legalized, "clear and emphatic opposition is a duty."[6]

Considerations insists, "any kind of formal cooperation in the enactment or application of such gravely unjust laws" and even any "material cooperation on the level of their application" must be avoided. "In this area, everyone can exercise the right to conscientious objection."[7]

LAWS FAVORING HOMOSEXUAL UNIONS
ARE CONTRARY TO RIGHT REASON

Indeed, "civil law cannot contradict right reason without losing its binding force on conscience. Every humanly-created law is legitimate insofar as it is consistent with the natural moral law, recognized by right reason, and insofar as it respects the inalienable rights of every person."[8]

Thus, "laws in favor of homosexual unions are contrary to right reason...the State could not grant legal standing to such

---

4. Ibid.
5. Ibid., no. 5.
6. Ibid.
7. Ibid.
8. Ibid., no. 6.

unions without failing in its duty to promote and defend marriage as an institution essential to the common good."[9]

LEGAL RECOGNITION PROMOTES
HOMOSEXUALITY AND WEAKENS MARRIAGE

Considerations refutes an objection often raised by the homosexual movement that, since the law allowing homosexual unions does not impose anything, it would not harm the common good.

> In this area, one needs first to reflect on the difference between homosexual behavior as a private phenomenon and the same behavior as a relationship in society, foreseen and approved by the law, to the point where it becomes one of the institutions in the legal structure. This second phenomenon is not only more serious, but also assumes a more wide-reaching and profound influence, and would result in changes to the entire organization of society, contrary to the common good. Civil laws are structuring principles of man's life in society, for good or for ill. They "play a very important and sometimes decisive role in influencing patterns of thought and behavior." Lifestyles and the underlying presuppositions these express not only externally shape the life of society, but also tend to modify the younger generation's perception and evaluation of forms of behavior. Legal recognition of homosexual unions would obscure certain basic moral values and cause a devaluation of the institution of marriage.[10]

---

9. Ibid.
10. Ibid.

NO ANALOGY BETWEEN SAME-SEX
UNIONS AND MARRIAGE

From a biological and anthropological standpoint, nature itself makes it impossible to even remotely compare any kind of homosexual union with marriage:

> Homosexual unions are totally lacking in the biological and anthropological elements of marriage and family which would be the basis, on the level of reason, for granting them legal recognition. Such unions are not able to contribute in a proper way to the procreation and survival of the human race.[11]

Resorting to artificial procreation does nothing to change this fact or make same-sex unions natural. Rather, it shows "a grave lack of respect for human dignity."[12] Same-sex unions are incapable of a real "conjugal dimension, which represents the human and ordered form of sexuality."[13]

HOMOSEXUAL ADOPTION:
A VIOLENCE TO INNOCENT CHILDREN

As for the adoption of children by homosexuals, *Considerations* very appropriately notes that it "would actually mean doing violence to these children," whose situation of weakness and dependence would place them "in an environment that is not conducive to their full human development." Besides being gravely immoral, adoption of children by homosexuals would violate the principle that "the weaker and more vulnerable party" must always be favored and protected.[14]

---

11. Ibid., no. 7.
12. Cf. Congregation for the Doctrine of the Faith, Instruction *Donum vitae* (Feb. 22, 1987), II. A. 1-3.
13. *Considerations*, no. 7.
14. Ibid.

Since the function of the State is to protect the weak, it must in this case defend children, rather than expose them to grave psychological and moral risks.

THE REDEFINITION OF MARRIAGE
WILL DESTROY SOCIETY

Considerations insists that society's survival is tied to a thriving family firmly established on marriage. It also points out the grave consequences to society if homosexual unions are legalized:

> The inevitable consequence of legal recognition of homosexual unions would be the redefinition of marriage, which would become, in its legal status, an institution devoid of essential reference to factors linked to heterosexuality; for example, procreation and raising children. If, from the legal standpoint, marriage between a man and a woman were to be considered just one possible form of marriage, the concept of marriage would undergo a radical trans-formation, with grave detriment to the common good. By putting homosexual unions on a legal plane anal-ogous to that of marriage and the family, the State acts arbitrarily and in contradiction with its duties.[15]

IT IS NOT UNJUST TO DENY
THAT WHICH IS NOT OWED IN JUSTICE

The homosexual movement claims that keeping same-sex unions illegal is discriminatory and a violation of justice since homosexuals are equally entitled to marriage and all its benefits.

---

15. Ibid., no. 8.

Considerations answers this sophism:

> Differentiating between persons or refusing social recognition or benefits is unacceptable only when it is contrary to justice. The denial of the social and legal status of marriage to forms of cohabitation that are not and cannot be marital is not opposed to justice; on the contrary, justice requires it.[16]

TRUE AUTONOMY NEVER HARMS THE COMMON GOOD

The Vatican document also refutes the autonomy argument used by the Supreme Court in the *Lawrence v. Texas* decision:

> Nor can the principle of the proper autonomy of the individual be reasonably invoked. It is one thing to maintain that individual citizens may freely engage in those activities that interest them and that this falls within the common civil right to freedom; it is something quite different to hold that activities which do not represent a significant or positive contribution to the development of the human person in society can receive specific and categorical recognition by the State. Not even in a remote analogous sense do homosexual unions fulfill the purpose for which marriage and family deserve specific categorical recognition. On the contrary, there are good reasons for holding that such unions are harmful to the proper development of human society, especially if their impact on society were to increase.[17]

---

16. Ibid.
17. Ibid.

CATHOLIC POLITICIANS NEED
TO BE CONSISTENT WITH THEIR FAITH

In its section "Positions of Catholic Politicians with Regard to Legislation in Favor of Homosexual Unions," *Considerations* emphasizes the obligation of Catholic politicians[18] to oppose such legislative proposals:

> If it is true that all Catholics are obliged to oppose the legalization of homosexual unions, Catholic politicians are obliged to do so in a particular way, in keeping with their responsibility as politicians.... The Catholic lawmaker has a moral duty to express his opposition clearly and publicly and to vote against it. To vote in favor of a law so harmful to the common good is gravely immoral.[19]

HOMOSEXUAL BEHAVIOR AND
UNIONS SIMPLY CANNOT BE APPROVED

Considerations emphasizes: "The Church teaches that respect for homosexual persons cannot lead in any way to approval of homosexual behavior or to considerations of homosexual unions."[20]

Thus, there can be no doubt that all Catholics have a duty to oppose the homosexual agenda. The Church's moral teaching cannot change.

---

18. Some Catholic politicians have invoked the secular principle of separation of Church and State as an excuse to shun Catholic morality in public life. What they are really doing is to separate, in themselves, the "Catholic" from the "politician." This separation violates the unity of being and the premises of morals and logic. Every man is judged by God according to his thoughts, words and deeds, and therefore, on the oneness of his personality.

19. *Considerations*, no. 10.

20. Ibid., no. 11.

The Ugandan Martyrs: Saints Charles Lwanga and Companions

The story of the Ugandan martyrs is a timely lesson for those opposed to homosexuality. It shows how with God's grace it is possible to resist fierce pressure to give in to homosexuality, even at the price of one's life.

At the end of the nineteenth century, a Catholic mission was established in Buganda, in what is now Uganda in Central Africa. The Faith was initially well received, but this changed under King Mwanga who persecuted the Church.

This tribal ruler used to sodomize the young pages serving in his court to satisfy his lust. While pagan, these young men submitted to his wishes, but, once they were baptized, they resisted the king, seeing his practices as gravely offensive to God's Law.

Joseph Mkasa had charge over the king's pages. As a Catholic, he did what he could to protect them from the king. The ruler reacted by beheading him on November 15, 1885. Charles Lwanga, also a Catholic, succeeded Joseph Mkasa and like him shielded the young victims.

King Mwanga's wrath knew no bounds. Perceiving that the faith was the root of the resistance, he resolved to exterminate it from the realm. He ordered the pages to be brought before him, and the Christians were set apart. Led by Lwanga, the Christian pages obeyed. Two other pages already under arrest joined them, as did two soldiers. The king asked them if they were determined to remain Christian. "Unto death," they answered. "Then kill them!" Some of the martyrs never made it to the place of execution, being speared or hacked to pieces along the way. The others endured the cruel death of being burnt alive. It was

Ascension Thursday, June 3, 1886.

Uganda's twenty-two martyrs were beatified in 1920 and solemnly canonized in 1964. Their feast is celebrated on June 3.

Conclusion

Joining moral issues like abortion, the homosexual debate now polarizes the nation. Should the homosexual movement succeed, it will force major changes in the laws and institutions of our country.

The debate, however, goes beyond mere legislation or social changes. When the Supreme Court's *Lawrence v. Texas* ruling turned morality in law upside down, it called into question our self-perception as "one nation under God."

Indeed, throughout our history, vast sectors of the American public have strongly identified with this religious perception. It permeates our culture. We inscribe it on our currency and embed it in our laws. As Americans, we are ingrained with the idea that God and His law have the right to be honored and obeyed, and that any nation that rejects this brings about its own ruin.

To forsake this perception is almost to renounce what it means to be American. It is to ask us to turn our backs on the values which have served so long to regulate our morality, guarantee public order and form the spiritual glue that unites God and country.

The move to impose homosexual marriage is now the spearhead of widespread efforts asking America to renounce this religious perception.

By essentially declaring in *Lawrence v. Texas* that the morality based on the Ten Commandments no longer has any legal standing, the Supreme Court joined radical liberals who are now clamoring for more: the proscription of any public acknowledgement of God and the expunging of morality from all law and culture.

This de-Christianizing of America is well advanced.

We see it, for example, in the wave of blasphemous plays, movies and "art" exhibits where God and His Holy Mother are dishonored, often at public institutions, and at taxpayer's expense. We see it in plays like *Corpus Christi*, where Our Lord is portrayed as "King of the Queers," or *The Most Fabulous Story Ever Told* with its Adam and Steve version of Genesis and its portrayal of the Blessed Virgin Mary as a lesbian.

We see it in attempts to suppress Christianity's freedom, squeezing it out of the public square, classrooms and even homes.

The victims could not be more innocent. A first-grade teacher in Sacramento County, California, says her principal has prohibited instructors from uttering the word "Christmas" in class or in written materials. A grade school boy in St. Louis is publicly reprimanded at school for bowing his head in prayer before meals. A Denver mother is told by a judge that the condition for her to retain custody of her daughter is not exposing her to "homophobic" Christian literature.

And now, even "under God" is wrenched from our Pledge of Allegiance and a monument to the Ten Commandments ignominiously wheeled away from Alabama's Supreme Court rotunda.

All this is done with an insensitivity that makes us wonder where are we headed?

Use this book to fight back, legally and peacefully. By exposing the religious, philosophical and scientific weaknesses of the homosexual movement, we can blunt the present spear-head of this broad anti-Christian offensive wherever it may appear. Use this book to educate fellow Americans about the false romantic myths the movement spreads about its lifestyle, its use of false compassion and its other sophistic arguments.

It is our hope that this work will strengthen the convictions of all who read it. Use the answers it presents in homes, workplaces and churches. May this book give courage to all who oppose the homosexual agenda.

This book is an appeal to the Ten Commandments America

to fearlessly reaffirm that God and His law have the supreme right to be honored and obeyed. It is especially a call to Catholics to take back the issue from those who hide behind false compassion. We must engage in this struggle using the Church's 2,000 years of strong, yet truly compassionate, opposition to homosexuality.

May Our Lady of the Immaculate Conception, Patroness of the United States, intercede with her Divine Son for America. May she bless maternally the efforts being made by so many, and may she grant victory to the nationwide effort to defend the sacred institutions of marriage and the family.

"When men resolve to cooperate with the grace of God, the marvels of history are worked: the conversion of the Roman Empire; the formation of the Middle Ages; the reconquest of Spain, starting from Covadonga; all the events that result from the great resurrections of soul of which peoples are also capable. These resurrections are invincible, because nothing can defeat a people that is virtuous and truly loves God."

Plinio Corrêa de Oliveira
Revolution and Counter-Revolution

APPENDIX

Are We Still "One Nation Under God"?

The Supreme Court's decision in
Lawrence v. Texas is America's "moral 9/11"

On June 26, 2003, the Supreme Court granted constitutional protection to sodomy.

In holding that a Texas law classifying sodomy as a misdemeanor violated the liberty protected under the Due Process Clause of the Fourteenth Amendment, the Supreme Court decriminalized sodomy nationwide, when practiced privately.

The case before the Court was *Lawrence v. Texas*. Many hailed the high court's decision as a *Roe v. Wade* for the homosexual movement. The analogy was well drawn. Both *Roe* and *Lawrence* are dark, tragic pages in our history.

America can be rightfully proud of its heroes and their feats of selfless dedication both at home and abroad. These represent glorious pages in our nation's history.

However, pages like *Roe* are shrouded in darkness. They obscure our glorious past and stain our honor. Consider the fact that *Roe* sealed the fate of some 44 million unborn Americans, a staggering figure equivalent to the combined populations of Montana, North Dakota, Minnesota, Wyoming, South Dakota, Illinois, Colorado, Nebraska, Iowa, Kansas, Missouri, Oklahoma and Arkansas.

1. AMERICA'S "MORAL 9/11"

Unlike *Roe*, *Lawrence* will not result directly in the killing of unborn Americans. However, it created the legal and psychological frameworks for the total destruction of what is left of the country's moral structures.

In one fell swoop the highest court in the land laid low the legal constructs of every state safeguarding public morality. *Lawrence* also paved the way for destroying a second set of

legal constructs—such as the country's many Defense of
Marriage Act (DOMA) laws—erected to protect the sacred
institutions of marriage and the family.

The scope of the Court's rationale in *Lawrence* is so broad
that it essentially affirms that there is no morality. As we see
it, *Lawrence* replicates in the moral realm the devastating
physical attack perpetrated against the nation on September
11, 2001.

2. AN INCREMENTAL APPROACH
THAT UNDERMINES PUBLIC MORALITY

The Supreme Court in *Lawrence* based its decision on a
string of cases that gradually expanded the right of privacy,
while denying the government's role in upholding public
morality.

Thus, in a first step, the Court held in 1965 that the Due
Process Clause established a right of privacy. This right of
privacy applied, the Court held, to the use of contraceptives by
married couples. It held further that the State had no right pass-
ing legislation infringing on this constitutional right (*Griswold
v. Connecticut*). In 1972, the Court used the Equal Protection
Clause to expand this interpretation of the right of privacy to
unmarried couples (*Eisenstadt v. Baird*). In 1973, the Court
used the Due Process Clause again to expand its interpretation
of the right of privacy to include abortion (*Roe v. Wade*).

The Supreme Court's 1986 decision in *Bowers v. Hardwick*
temporarily interrupted the trend. *Bowers* affirmed sodomy
was not a fundamental right, and that there was a legitimate
state interest to make it a crime.

By overturning *Bowers* in *Lawrence*, the Supreme Court
continued its incremental approach, profoundly undermining
public morality.

The next step in this gradualist reshaping of public morality is the legal and social acceptance of "marriage" between homosexuals[1] and their adoption of children. The Supreme Court will be no obstacle.[2]

3. A CLEAR RUPTURE WITH 2,000 YEARS OF CHRISTIAN TRADITION

The Supreme Court chided the justices who decided *Bowers* for allowing themselves to be swayed by the moral standards formed during the 2,000-year history of Western Christian civilization, instead of hearkening to "the emerging awareness that liberty gives substantial protection to adult persons in deciding how to conduct their private lives in matters pertaining to sex."

"*Bowers* was making the broader point," *Lawrence* reads, "that for centuries there have been powerful voices to condemn homosexual conduct as immoral. The condemnation has been shaped by religious beliefs, conceptions of right and acceptable behavior, and respect for the traditional family. For many persons these are not trivial concerns but profound and deep convictions accepted as moral and ethical principles to which they aspire and which thus determine the course of their lives."

The Court in *Lawrence* solemnly reaffirmed its decisions in previous cases to break with this Christian heritage and stated

---

1. As much as possible we avoid using the word gay, as its generalized use would be a victory, in our view, for homosexual ideology. Indeed, the word itself connotes joy. A vice that is an aberration against nature cannot give true joy or happiness. Likewise, in opposition to a usage that is becoming generalized, we restrict the term *homosexuality* to homosexual practices, thus excluding the mere inclination. No individual who suffers from such an unnatural inclination and resists it with the help of grace can be called a homosexual, just as no one who resists the inclination to steal or lie can be called a thief or a liar.

2. *Lawrence* opens wide the door to homosexual "marriage." The Court stated: "When sexuality finds overt expression in intimate conduct with another person, the conduct can be but one element in a ***personal bond that is more enduring***. The liberty protected by the Constitution allows homosexual persons the right to make this choice" (emphasis added).

that, for it, "our laws and traditions in the past half century are of most relevance here."

4. LIBERTY BECOMES LICENSE WHEN IT BREAKS AWAY FROM NATURAL AND DIVINE LAW

Bowers had to be overturned, the Court stated, because it failed "to appreciate the extent of the liberty at stake." "Liberty presumes an autonomy of self,"[3] and the Court's duty is "to define the liberty of all."[4]

Thus, the "right to liberty" was the basis for the Court's decision to grant constitutional protection to sodomy.

The Court's discussion as to how "liberty" is to be understood, although of paramount importance given *Lawrence*'s far-reaching consequences, was grossly inadequate.

As the Fourteenth Amendment reminds us, a person can be imprisoned—thus losing his *personal* liberty—only after due process of law. It is openly debatable if the Fourteenth Amendment deals with *moral* liberty. Nevertheless, an erroneous concept of moral liberty is at the heart of the Court's decision in *Lawrence*.

Moral liberty is not meant to subsist in a vacuum. It must be understood within the framework of a moral order, within the context of a moral natural law that itself is anchored in the eternal law established by the Creator and which governs the order of the universe. When moral liberty is detached from natural and divine law it soon degenerates into license. As Pope Leo XIII reminds us in the Encyclical *Libertas*:

---

3. "Persons in a homosexual relationship may seek autonomy for these purposes, just as heterosexual persons do. The decision in *Bowers* would deny them this right."
4. The Court reiterated its holding in *Planned Parenthood of Southeastern Pennsylvania v. Casey* that "our obligation is to define the liberty of all, not to mandate our own moral code."

Liberty, the highest of natural endowments, being the portion only of intellectual or rational natures, confers on man this dignity—that he is 'in the hand of his counsel'[5] and has power over his actions. But the manner in which such dignity is exercised is of the greatest moment, inasmuch as on the use that is made of liberty the highest good and the greatest evil alike depend. Man, indeed, is free to obey his reason, to seek moral good, and to strive unswervingly after his last end. Yet he is free also to turn aside to all other things; and, in pursuing the empty semblance of good, to disturb rightful order and to fall headlong into the destruction which he has voluntarily chosen....

Therefore, the nature of human liberty, however it be considered, whether in individuals or in society, whether in those who command or in those who obey, supposes the necessity of obedience to some supreme and eternal law, which is no other than the authority of God, commanding good and forbidding evil. And, so far from this most just authority of God over men diminishing, or even destroying their liberty, it protects and perfects it, for the real perfection of all creatures is found in the prosecution and attainment of their respective ends, but the supreme end to which human liberty must aspire is God.

In contrast, *Lawrence* allows so broad an interpretation of "liberty," that all state laws proscribing evils such as prostitution, adultery, bigamy, incest, sadomasochism,

---

5. Ecclus. 15:14.
6. *The Papal Encyclicals, 1878-1903*, Claudia Carlen, I.H.M., ed. (New York: McGrath Publishing Company, 1981), p. 169.

pedophilia, and bestiality are now at risk.

5. GOVERNMENT HAS NO RIGHT TO RENOUNCE ITS NATURAL LAW DUTY TO UPHOLD MORALITY IN THE PURSUIT OF THE COMMON GOOD

The Court ascribed much importance to decisions by the European Court of Human Rights and the fact that many countries have legalized sodomy.[7] It then concluded that "there has been no showing that in this country the governmental interest in circumscribing personal choice is somehow more legitimate or urgent."

The Court focused on the "right to liberty," when it was duty bound to base its decision first and foremost on the responsibility of every political authority (including the judiciary) to uphold that most fundamental principle of natural law:[8] "Do good and avoid evil."

This does not mean that the State must enforce the practice of every virtue and proscribe the indulgence in every vice, as attempted by the ayatollahs of our days. Rather, it means that in legislating on moral matters, which it should do only when these directly affect the common good, it must legislate so as

---

7. "Other nations, too, have taken action consistent with an affirmation of the protected right of homosexual adults to engage in intimate, consensual conduct. The right the petitioners seek in this case has been accepted as an integral part of human freedom in many other countries."

8. "Natural moral law and its component part, the *ius naturale*, is precisely this divine law with reference to man, so far as the latter participates in the divine law. The eternal law dwells as blind necessity in irrational nature. As oughtness, as norm of free moral activity, it is inscribed in the heart of man, a rational and free being.... There is no soul, however corrupt it may be, in whose conscience God does not speak, if only it is still capable of rational thought. There are human actions, consequently, which are in themselves good or bad. Bad acts are not qualified as such by force of law, but because they are such in themselves: because they constitute a disturbance of the natural order.... Not the will of the earthly lawgiver, but variance with natural reason is the ground of the intrinsic immorality of determinate actions" (Heinrich A. Rommen, *The Natural Law: A Study in Legal and Social History and Philosophy* [St. Louis: B. Herder Book Company, 1947], pp. 37-38).

to favor virtue, and raise obstacles to vice.

Nevertheless, in circumstances where homosexuality is indeed advancing worldwide, how are Americans to construe *Lawrence*? Seeing how sodomy was converted from its legal status as a crime in some states into a constitutionally protected form of "liberty," how can they construe the Court's action except as favoring not virtue, but unnatural vice?

This dereliction of duty represents a major blow to America's Christian roots, the institution of the family and the very foundation of morality and society.

6. SACRED SCRIPTURE AND CHURCH TEACHING CONDEMN HOMOSEXUALITY

As stated, the Supreme Court chastises *Bowers* for upholding centuries of legal precedent shaped by natural law and Christian doctrine.

Centuries after *Lawrence*'s reversal, after it has become no more than a footnote for American history experts, homosexuality will continue to be condemned by Sacred Scripture and the Catholic Church.

Indeed, homosexuality is a sin condemned in both the Old and the New Testaments.[9] Saint Peter in his Second Epistle, for example, says:

> And reducing the cities of the Sodomites, and of the Gomorrhites, into ashes, God condemned them to be overthrown, making them an example to those that should afterwards act wickedly. And He delivered just Lot, oppressed by the injustice and lewd conversation of the wicked (2:6-7).

---

9. Cf. Gen. 19:1-29; Lev. 18:22; Deut. 22:5; 2 Pet. 2:6-7; Rom. 1:24-27; 1 Cor. 6:9-10.

In his Epistle to the Romans, Saint Paul says:

> Wherefore God gave them up to the desires of their heart, unto uncleanness, to dishonor their own bodies among themselves.
>
> Who changed the truth of God into a lie; and worshiped and served the creature rather than the Creator, who is blessed for ever. Amen.
>
> For this cause God delivered them up to shameful affections. For their women have changed the natural use into that use which is against nature.
>
> And, in like manner, the men also, leaving the natural use of the women, have burned in their lusts one towards another, men with men working that which is filthy, and receiving in themselves the recompense which was due to their error (1:24-27).

Homosexuality has also been condemned by Fathers and Doctors of the Church, and by the Popes for 2,000 years. Saint Peter Damian, Doctor of the Church, for example, says it "should not be considered an ordinary vice, for it surpasses all of them in enormity."[10]

The Catechism of St. Pius X calls homosexuality a sin that "cries out to Heaven for vengeance,"[11] and the *Catechism of the Catholic Church* promulgated by Pope John Paul II in 1992 says: "Basing itself on Sacred Scripture, which presents homosexual acts as acts of grave depravity, tradition has always declared that 'homosexual acts are intrinsically disordered.'"[12]

---

10. *The Book of Gomorrah* (*Patrologia Latina*, vol. 145, col. 159-190) quoted in Roberto de Mattei, *L'Église et l'homosexualité* (Paris: Pierre Téqui Éditeur, 1995), p. 12.

11. www.ewtn.com/library/catechism/PiusXCat.txt. Theologians give Gen. 19:13 as the scriptural basis for this designation.

12. *Catechism of the Catholic Church* (New York: Doubleday, 1995) § 2357, p. 625.

And in his February 20, 1994 Angelus Address, protesting against a special resolution of the European Parliament encouraging the nations of Europe to approve homosexual "marriage," Pope John Paul II states:

> What is not morally acceptable, however, is the legalization of homosexual acts. To show understanding towards the person who sins, towards the person who is not in the process of freeing himself from this tendency, does not at all mean to diminish the demands of the moral norm (cf. *Veritatis Splendor*, 95)....
>
> But we must say that what was intended with the European Parliament's resolution was the legitimization of a moral disorder. Parliament improperly conferred an institutional value to a conduct that is deviant and not in accordance with God's plan....
>
> Forgetting the words of Christ '*The truth shall set you free*' (John 8:32), an attempt was made to show the people of our continent a moral evil, a deviance, a certain slavery, as a form of liberation, falsifying the very essence of the family.[13]

True charity towards homosexuals consists in showing them the enormous unnatural lie they have embraced, to help them see the horror of the sin in which they find themselves, and to assist them in every way to abandon their deplorable state.

7. CAN WE STILL SEE OURSELVES AS "ONE NATION UNDER GOD"?

An act is immoral if it violates natural or divine law. That an

---

13. Angelus Address of February 20, 1994, at www.vatican.va/holy_father/ john_paul_ii/angelus/1994/documents/hf_jp-ii_ang_19940220_it.html. (Our translation from the Italian original.)

immoral act is committed in private does not diminish the fact that it still offends God, for no sin, private or otherwise, escapes His omniscience. Not even our most intimate thoughts are unknown to Him.

In civil society, it behooves the State to punish immoral acts—including those practiced privately—that harm the common good and disturb the social order. Homosexuality, incest, and other sexual abnormalities undermine the family, which is the basis of society.

To sustain that it is not a legitimate state interest to punish homosexual acts that are practiced privately is tantamount to affirming that it is not in the State's interest to protect the family and, therefore, the common good.

Moreover, when the State's condoning of such immoral acts is codified into positive law, the latter breaks with natural and divine law. In so doing, as Saint Thomas Aquinas teaches, positive law perverts itself.[14] In breaking with the eternal law, the State establishes a new atheistic standard of "morality."

The day America subscribes to this atheistic "morality," how can it continue to ask for God's blessings with any sincerity of heart? How can it honestly refer to itself in the Pledge of Allegiance as "one nation under God"?

8. WE SHOULD FEAR THAT GOD WILL WITHDRAW HIS BLESSINGS FROM AMERICA

America is a profoundly religious nation. Even today,

---

14. "As Augustine says (De Lib. Arb. i, 5) 'that which is not just seems to be no law at all': wherefore the force of a law depends on the extent of its justice. Now in human affairs a thing is said to be just, from being right, according to the rule of reason. But the first rule of reason is the law of nature, as is clear from what has been stated above (Q. 91, Art. 2 ad 2). Consequently every human law has just so much of the nature of law, as it is derived from the law of nature. But if in any point it deflects from the law of nature, it is no longer a law but a perversion of law" (*The "Summa Theologica" of St. Thomas Aquinas*, II-I, Q. 95, Art. 2 [London: R. & T. Washbourne, Ltd., 1915], pp. 56-57).

amidst the raging Cultural War, when religion is being slowly squeezed out of the public square, it finds refuge in the depths of many hearts.

While many in Europe deride the fact that our political leaders, especially after 9/11, weave quotes from Scripture into their speeches and end them with "God bless America," we actually love the custom.

God has blessed our nation abundantly in its short history and it is proper and good that we express our gratitude.

Will America continue to receive God's blessings in the wake of *Lawrence*? We certainly hope and pray that it will.

This will certainly happen, if Americans resolve to reject the homosexual agenda[15] despite the pressure brought to bear by a liberal media, the world of Hollywood, and more unwanted changes to our laws by the Supreme Court.

9. THOSE WHO LOVE GOD NEED TO STAND UP AND BE COUNTED

Genesis teaches us that God was determined to punish Sodom and Gomorrah for their wicked ways. Abraham begged for mercy, asking God if He intended to destroy the just with the wicked. He asked God if He would punish Sodom if there were even fifty just men in the city. God replied: "If I find in

---

15. Livio Melina, professor of moral theology at the Pontifical Lateran University of Rome, makes an important observation on "gay culture": "Today this term [*gay*] is highly politicized and does not simply mean a homosexually oriented person but one who publicly adopts a homosexual 'lifestyle' and is committed to having it accepted by society as fully legitimate. Justifiable opposition to offences and discrimination, which violate a person's basic rights, cannot be confused with this demand. In fact a systematic plan for the public justification and glorification of homosexuality is taking shape, starting with the attempt to make it fully accepted in the mind of society. It aims, through increasing pressure, at a change in legislation so that homosexual unions may enjoy the same rights as marriage, including that of adoption" ("Christian Anthropology and Homosexuality: Moral criteria for evaluating homosexuality," *L'Osservatore Romano*, weekly English edition, March 12, 1997, p.5).

Sodom fifty just men, I will spare the whole place for their sake."[16] Abraham knew there were not fifty just men in Sodom so he bargained with God. What if only forty-five could be found? What if only forty? Or thirty? Twenty? Ten? The Lord said: "I will not destroy it for the sake of ten."[17]

Here is a lesson for us today. If we love America, and we do, we must stand up and be counted by God. He must be able to find enough faithful souls who abide by His Commandments.

We may or may not be able to reverse *Lawrence* in the short run, but we must work untiringly to create the moral climate whereby homosexuality is rejected. We must not be intimidated. We must voice our rejection loudly and firmly, legally and peacefully, in defense of Christian morals. Only such public voicing of our rejection of the homosexual agenda can ascend to Heaven as a worthy act of reparation to our offended God.

We can prove ourselves true to God. We know that we can stand by Our Lord not just during His many miracles, when He cured the sick and raised the dead. We know that we can stand by Him not only amid the public acclaim of Palm Sunday.

We know that we can be right there next to Him when He is nailed to the Cross. Right there close to the Blessed Virgin Mary, Saint John and the holy women, amid the taunts and jeers, even if all we can do is to proclaim His innocence and our faith in Him like the Good Thief: "Lord, remember me when You shall come into Your kingdom."[18]

We are Americans. We believe in liberty. True liberty! There is no power on earth that can make us change, unless we *choose*.

May God bless America!

July 4, 2003
The American TFP

---

16. Gen. 18:26.
17. Gen. 18:32.
18. Luke 23:42.

INDEX

a Lapide, Cornelius, 131-132, 150-151

Abortion, 14, 28, 71, 187, 192

Adoption, by homosexuals, 181

Adultery, 11, 28, 69, 98, 99, 143, 148n., 156, 169, 195

After the Ball, 31ff., 60, 123

AIDS, 31, 34, 71, 107n., 109-110, 113-114

Alcohol and drug abuse, 110-113

Alphonsus Liguori, Saint, 68n., 71n., 153n.

America, *Ten Commandments*, 2-3, 188; -'s "moral 9/11," 191; *Middle*, 32-33, 37, 39

American Federation of Teachers/National Gay and Lesbian Caucus, 26n.

American Psychiatric Association, 23, 88

American Society for the Defense of Tradition, Family and Property, The (see Tradition, Family and Property)

American Sociological Association, 107

Anarchy, 1n., 2, 13, 61, 82, 145, 146

Androgyny, 7, 54-56, 61-63

Animal "homosexuality," 89-93

Aquinas, Saint Thomas, 67n., 68n., 69n., 72n., 74, 77, 77n., 78, 78n., 79, 79n., 80n., 82n., 95n., 119, 119n., 153n., 160, 161n., 200, 200n.

Athenagoras of Athens, 155

Augustine, Saint, xvi, 74, 95n., 121, 158, 200n.

Bailey, J. Michael, 83, 85, 86

Berdache, 56, 60

Bernardine of Siena, Saint, 162

Bestiality, 50, 134, 169, 196

Bigamy, 195

Blasphemy, 109n., 155, 167, 187

Bowers v. Hardwick, 21, 192-194, 197

Bracket technique, 36

Bridget, Jan, 112-113

Bronski, Michael, 56-57

Buela, Fr. Carlos Miguel, 73-75

Byrd, A. Dean, 40n., 85-86

Call to Action, 27

Campus PrideNet, 25

Catechism of the Catholic Church, 67n., 176, 179, 198

Catherine of Siena, Saint, 161-162

Catholic Medical Association, 83, 84n., 88

Celebrities, endorsement for the homosexual lifestyle, 34, 38

Celibacy, 103

Centers for Disease Control and Prevention (CDC), 109, 113

Charles Lwanga and Companions, Saints, 185-186

Chastity, xv, 11, 14, 67, 71, 103, 151, 156, 170-172, 176, 178-179

Chittister, Sr. Joan, 105-106, 111

Christian civilization, xv, 3, 11, 56n., 193

Christianity, 4, 11n., 56, 57, 58, 60, 61, 62, 153, 155, 188

Church, 101,102, 103, 155-
159,161; *not tainted by sin,*
147n; *persecuted in Uganda
by homosexual ruler,* 186ff.;
separation of - and State,
184n.; *teaching on homosexuality,* 26, 27, 29, 30, 95, 137ff.,
147ff., 155, 156, 165ff, 172,
173ff., 184, 189, 197-198;
teaching on sexuality, 173;
*why Our Lord allows crises in
the,* 147n.

Civil law, cannot contradict
right reason, 179

Civil rights, 8-9,34,100

Civil unions, 3, 43, 95

Clark, J. Michael, 55-56

Clinton, President Bill, 24

Code of Canon Law (1917),
165, 168-170

Code of Canon Law (1983),
170-171

Communism, 16-20

Compassion, xv, 36, 109, 176;
false concept of, 117ff., 178,
188, 189; *manipulation of,*
122; *true,* 121; *virtue of,* 119-
120

Conference of Catholic
Lesbians, Inc., 27

Congregation for the Doctrine
of the Faith, 101, 117n., 173-
174, 177, 181n.

Congregation for the Religious,
171

Conscience, 90n., 139-140, 142,
145, 177, 179, 196n.

*Considerations Regarding
Proposals to Give Legal*

*Recognition to Unions
Between Homosexual Persons,*
101n., 117, 177

Contraception, 28, 71, 175; *the
"pill,"* 12, 13

Conversion, 8, 32, 61, 121, 158,
189

Council, *of Ancyra,* 165n.; *of
Elvira,* 165; *of Nablus,* 165n.;
of Paris, 165n.; *of Rheims,*
165n.; *of Toledo,* XVI 165n.;
of Trosly, 165n.; *Lateran III,*
166; *Lateran V,* 166, 167; *of
Tours II,* 165n.; *Vatican II,* 73-
76

Crowley, Aleister, 17, 55

Culpepper, Emily, 55

Cultural war, xvi, 2-3, 32, 35,
39, 62, 122, 201

Culture, 2-3, 11-12, 14-15, 25,
39, 53, 61, 64, 86, 89, 148,
187, 201n.

Cyprian of Carthage, Saint, 59

Davenport, Katherine, 20n.

Defense of Marriage Act
(DOMA), 192

*Diagnosis and Statistical
Manual* (DSM-III), homosexuality excluded from, 24

Dignity (Catholic homosexual
organization), 27, 87n., 118

Discrimination, against homosexuality, 8, 23, 27, 34, 102,
176, 201n.

DNA research and "gay gene,"
83n., 86

Domestic partnerships, 3, 8, 43,
95

Dostoevsky, Feodor

Mikhailovich, 145
Ecclesiastical discipline on homosexuality, 165ff.
Eighner, Lars, 109
Entertainment, world of, *influenced by the homosexual movement*, 21, 25, 105; *obsession with sexuality*, 11
Eusebius of Cæesarea, 156
Evans, Arthur, 35
Falwell, Jerry, 8n.
Family, *traditional*, 193; *defense of*, xv, 3, 39, 189, 192; *erosion of*, 14, 28; *established on marriage*, 181-183; *foundation of society*, 197; *God's plan for*, 178; *right to constitute*, 99; *undermined by homosexuality*, 81-82, 97-98, 199, 200
Fashion, *and androgyny*, 18, 53, 62; *and sexual revolution*, 11; *influence of*, 53n.
Feldblum, Chai, 77
Feminism, 12, 53, 55n.
Fornication, 28, 68n., 69, 135, 155
Foucault, Michel, 54-55
Fourteenth Amendment, 191, 194
Fox, Tom, 118
Freud, Sigmund, 13n.
Friendship, destroyed by homosexuality, 81-82
Garry, Joan, 25
Gaudium et Spes, 73-76
Gay & Lesbian Alliance Against Defamation (GLAAD), 25, 41
Gay Activists Alliance (GAA), 35

Gay and Lesbian Medical Association, 113
Gay and Lesbians Working in Education, 26n.
Gay gene, 83, 86
Gay, Lesbian and Straight Teachers Network, 26n.
Gay-Straight Alliance, 119
Georgetown University, 28-30
Gernreich, Rudi, 18
Gnosis, 16, 61, 62-64,154
Goldsmith, Tom, 119
Gomorrah, 123ff., 147, 157, 167, 201
Goodridge v. Dept. of Public Health, 3, 21
Gramick, Sr. Jeannine, 118
Green, Thomas J., 171
Gregory IX, Pope, 166
Gregory the Great, Pope Saint, 151, 158
Hamer, Dean, 83, 86
Hay, Harry, 14-20, 54, 56-58, 60-62, 64
Hefner, Hugh, 12
Hermaphroditism (see also Androgyny), 54, 55n., 61n., 154
Hervada, Javier, 75-76
HIV (see also AIDS), 107n., 110, 113, 114
Hollywood, 12, 16, 56, 105, 111, 201
Homophile, xvi, 18
Homophobia, 35-36, 188
Homosexual, **acts**: *and sterility*, 101; *intrinsically disordered*, 27, 176, 178-179, 198; *contrary to the common good*, 200; *contrary to natural moral*

law, 178; *gravely contrary to chastity*, 176, 179; **agenda**: xv, xvii, 4, 24, 36, 43, 87, 95, 117, 184, 188, 202; **behavior**: *and deviant forms of sexual behavior*, 50; *animal*, 89ff.; *cannot be approved*, 184; *possibility of change*, 87-89; **ideology**: 43, 47, 53-54, 56, 62, 77, 106, 123, 178, 179, 193n.; **inclination/tendency (see also same-sex attraction)**: xv-xvii, 49, 107, 172, 174, 176, 199; *an objective disorder*, 174, 176, 179, 193n.; **lifestyle**: *celebrities endorsement for the,* 34, 38, 109-110; *promiscuity of the,* 109; *romanticised,* 4, 105-106; *and violence*, 110-11; **love**: *impossibility of,* 77ff., 80-81; **promiscuity**: 31, 109ff.; **unions**: 25, 44, 177-184, 201n.

Homosexual movement, **antagonism between the - and Christianity**: 62; **influence**: *on education*, 25-26; *the media*, 25; *politics and legislation*, 23-25; *religion*, 26-27; **international scope**, 22-23; **origins**, 15ff.; **pagan androgyny**, 55, 62; **tactics**, 31-41, 123

Homosexual network, 16, 21ff.
Homosexual revolution, 11, 14, 15, 17, 21, 22, 39, 111, 177
Homosexuality and Hope, 83, 84n., 87n., 88, 89n.,
Human rights, 34, 99

Human Rights Campaign, 23, 24, 41
Human Sexuality - New Directions in American Catholic Thought, 124-125, 133-134
I Have Weathered Other Storms, 147n., 151n.
Impurity, 71n., 108, 149, 150, 151, 161
Incest, 69, 97, 134, 143, 148, 169, 195, 200
Initiation, 15, 58n.
Instruction: Careful Selection and Training of Candidates for the States of Perfection and Sacred Orders, 171-172
Int'l Assoc. of Lesbian, Gay, Bisexual, Transgendered Pride Coordinators, Inc., (see InterPride)
InterPride, 22; *anti-Catholic views*, 23
Irenaeus of Lyons, Saint, 154
Jerome, Saint, 130, 131, 153n., 156
John Chrysostom, Saint, 131, 157
John Paul II, Pope, 97n., 153n., 170, 175, 198, 199
John the Apostle, Saint, 77, 154, 202
Jones, Peter, 55, 56n.
Jude the Apostle, Saint, 126, 127, 128n., 132, 147
Justin, Saint, 153, 154
Kight, Morris, 20
Kinsey Report, 40
Kirk, Marshall, 31-39, 46, 60, 61, 82n., 108, 109n., 123

Lambda Legal Defense and Education Fund (Lambda Legal), 24, 44

Lang, Helmut, 53

Latkovic, Mark S., 73

Lawrence v. Texas, 1-3, 21, 24, 28, 41, 43, 183, 187, 191ff.

Legalization of same-sex "marriage," 43, 98, 118, 177, 179, 184, 199

Legislation in favor of homosexual unions, *obligation to oppose*, 184; *to protect a condemnable behavior*, 175; *homosexual influence on*, 23, 201n.; Lawrence v. Texas, *the end of all morals legislation*, 2

Legislative, homosexual offensive, 23, 177

Leo XIII, Pope, 96n., 194-195

Lesbian Information Service, 112

Letter to the Bishops of the Catholic Church on the Pastoral Care of Homosexual Persons, 174-175

LeVay, Simon, 83-85

Liberty, *absolute, and atheistic and anarchic morality*, 2; *as the supreme norm of human thought and action*, 1, 2; *limits of human*, 96, 143, 194ff.; *moral*, 143, 194

Lot, 126, 129, 131, 135, 163, 197

Love, *of desire*, 78, 79; *of friendship*, 78, 79, 80; *an end of matrimony*, 68n., 73-76, 102; *conjugal*, 68n., 70, 73-76, 80-81, 106; *different forms of*, 78; *for the sinner*, xvi, 120; *impossibility of homosexual*, 77ff., 80-81; *nature of true*, 78-79; *romantic*, 11

LSD, 111

Madsen, Hunter, 31-39, 46, 60, 61, 82n., 108, 109n., 123

Marriage (see also Matrimony), *and the common good*, 98, 180; *and same-sex "marriage,"* 98, 106, 115; *and sexual revolution*, 14; *and sterility*, 101, 189; *between a girl and a dog*, 98n.; *Christian*, 70; *defense of*, xv, 3; *ends of*, 73-76, 102; *civil unions have no analogy with*, 181; *redefinition of - destroys society*, 182; *right to*, 45-46; *solely between a man and a woman*, 177-178; *weakened by homosexuality*, 180

Marriage Equality USA, 46

Marriage Protection Week 2003, 25

Marx, Karl, 13n.

Marxism, 16, 17, 19

Massachusetts Supreme Judicial Court, 3, 21

Matrimony (see also Marriage), *elevation to supernatural level*, 70; *ends of*, 73-76

Mattachine Society, 15, 17ff., 54, 57

Media, 17, 21, 25, 34, 35, 43, 83, 87n., 98n., 105, 173, 201

Middle Ages, 18, 166, 189

Middle America, 32, 33, 37, 39

Minority, *oppressed*, 23; *homo-*

sexuals as a, 17, 21
Modesty, 11, 14, 131, 156
Monica, Saint, 121
Monogamy 68; *myth of homo-
sexual*, 106-108
Moral revolution, 7ff., 49, 51,
62
Mysticism, erotic, 4, 53ff., 61,
62
National Consortium of Dir-
ectors of Lesbian Gay Bisex-
ual and Transgender Resources
in Higher Education, 25
National Educational Associa-
tion's Gay and Lesbian
Caucus, 26n.
National Gay and Lesbian Task
Force (NGLTF), 8n., 23, 24n.,
40, 41
National Institute of Mental
Health, 114
Natural law, xv, 1, 2, 4, 29,
35, 36, 45, 47, 56, 59, 67,
68n., 75, 95, 96, 97, 100, 106,
137, 139-144, 163, 173, 175,
176, 194, 196, 197
Natural moral law, 103, 139,
141, 173, 175, 178, 179, 196n.
Neopaganism, 4, 20, 57, 60, 61,
62
New American Bible, 125-127,
130, 132
New Dictionary of Theology,
124, 130
New Ways Ministry, 27
Nicolosi, Joseph, 108n.
North American Man/Boy Love
Association (NAMBLA), 16n.,
20, 32

Nugent, Fr. Robert, 118
Occultism, 16, 61
Oliveira, Plinio Corrêa de, 14n.,
17n., 21, 53n., 189
"One nation under God," 4, 29,
187, 191, 199, 200
Order of the Eastern Temple, 16
Paganism (see also Neopagan-
ism), 55, 57, 59, 61, 148, 153,
185; *sexual ideal*, 55; *androgy-
ny, - and the homosexual
movement*, 55
Parades (marches), homosexual,
20, 22, 23, 24, 32, 37, 43, 56n.
Partnership benefits, 3, 8
Paul the Apostle, Saint, xv, 69,
70, 103, 108, 134, 142, 145,
147ff.
Pederasty, 50, 147n., 172
Pedophilia, 40, 50, 100, 196
Persuasion, to change position
on homosexuality, 31, 39
Peter Canisius, Saint, 163
Peter Damian, Saint, 159-160,
198
Peter the Apostle, Saint, 135,
147, 163, 197
Pillard, Richard C., 83, 85, 86
Pius V, Pope Saint, 166-168
Pius X, Pope Saint, 168, 198
Pius XI, Pope, 74, 102
Pius XII, Pope, 73, 75, 100n.
Playboy magazine, and the
sexual revolution, 12
Pledge of Allegiance, 188, 200
Politicians, Catholic, 176, 177,
182, 184; *homosexual pressure
on*, 40; *supported by homosex-
ual organizations*, 24

Polygamy, 97

Pornography, 14, 28, 71, 98, 100

Pre-marital sexual intercourse, 173, 175

Pride, *first among the vices of Sodom*, 130, 163; *source of impurity*, 150-151

Privacy, 97, 192

Procreation, *and conjugal love*, 80; *and homosexuality*, 101, 132, 181-182; *and the ends of marriage*, 45, 73-76, 102; *gnostics against*, 63; *instinct of - and temperance*, 78; *main purpose of sexual intercourse*, 68; *separation of sexual activity from*, 13

Promiscuity 14, 31; *among homosexuals*, 109-110; *and sexually transmitted diseases (STD)*, 113-114

Propaganda war, 34, 38, 39, 40

Prostitution, 11, 71, 98, 148, 154, 195; *ritual*, 59; *child*, 97

Psychological dependency, *homosexuality and*, 81; *therapy*, 87

Public health, 109, 111

Public morality, *complete inversion of*, 8; *declining standards of*, 4; *homosexuality undermining*, 97; *the State and the safeguard of*, 46, 97, 191-192; *undermined by* Lawrence v. Texas, 191-192

Purity, 14, 59, 151

Radical Faeries, 20, 56-60

Rainbow Sash Movement USA (National Organization of Gay/Lesbian/Bisexual/Transgender Catholics), 27, 118n., 117

Rainbow warriors, 21

Reich, Charles, 13n.

Reich, Wilhem, 13n.

Religion, *important motive for abandoning homosexuality*, 88

Religious war, 62

Renaissance, 7, 18n.

Revolution and Counter-Revolution, 14n., 21n., 53n., 189

Ritual prostitution 59; *homosexual neopagan*, 57-60; *occultist*, 16

Roe v. Wade, 191, 192

Romanticism, *and the homosexual lifestyle*, 4, 105-106, 188; *philosophical and religious implications of*, 11n.; *and the sexual revolution*, 11-12; *and distortion of friendship*, 79

Rondeau, Paul E., 39 n.

Roscoe, Will, 56n., 61n., 64n.

Rueda, Fr. Enrique T., 22

Sade, Marquis of, 108-109

Sadism, 32, 50, 109, 195

Same-sex attraction, *not a synonym for homosexuality*, xvii; *not genetic*, 83-86; *not irreversible*, 87-89; *therapy for*, 88-89; *spiritual solution for*, 175

Same-sex "marriage," 8; *granting constitutional protection to*, 1; *and the homosexual offensive*, 3; *and the homosexual ideology*, 43, 77; *is not*

marriage, 44; *sentimental arguments in favor of*, 46; *versus traditional marriage*, 98; *sophistic arguments in favor of*, 95ff.
Santorum, Senator Rick, 8n
Sartre, Jean-Paul, 145-146
Saslow, James M., 7n
Satanism, 17
Schmidt, Thomas E., 109, 111, 112n
Schneider, Margaret, 53
Schumacher, Brenda, 108
Secor, Laura, 21, 43, 77n
Selling Homosexuality to America, 39
Sexual act, purpose of, 67ff., 96, 160-161
Sexual liberation, 9, 14, 31, 53
Sexual magic rituals, 55
Sexual revolution, 11-14, 20, 53, 173
Sexually transmitted diseases (STD), 71, 110, 113
Shamans, homosexuals and lesbians as, 55
Sin, *against chastity*, 67, 170; *homosexuality, a grave*, 178; *against nature*, 160-161; *that "cries out to heaven for vengeance,"* 123, 135, 198; *Original*, 11n., 69-70, 77
Socarides, Charles W., 22
Sodom, 123-135, 147, 156-157, 159, 163, 167, 201-202
Sommer, Susan, 24
Soulforce, 26
Southern California Gay Liberation Front, 20

Spitzer, Robert L., 88
Sterility, 68n, 101
Stonewall riots, 20
Suicide, and homosexuality, 8, 110, 114-115
Sullivan, Andrew, 95n.
Supreme Court (United States), 1-3, 21, 24, 28, 43, 183, 187-188, 191-193, 197, 201
Synod, *of Angers*, 165n; *of Beziers*, 165n; *of Paris*, 165n; *of Rouen*, 165n.
Taparelli D'Azeglio, S.J., Fr. Luigi, 100, 100n.
Teachers Group, 26n.
Temperance, virtue of, 11, 78-79, 160
Ten Commandments, 2-4, 36, 47, 133, 143, 187-188
Ten percent myth, 40-41
Tertullian, 153n, 156
TFP Student Action, 28-30
Therapy, *homosexual opposition to cure/change*, 8, 87; *successful in effecting behavioral and attractional change*, 87-89
Thérèse of the Child Jesus, Saint, 153n
Thomas Aquinas, Saint (see Aquinas)
Thorstad, David, 20n
Timmons, Stuart, 15-20, 56n, 57n, 58
Tobacco, higher use by homosexuals, 111-112
Topless dresses, 18
Tradition, Family and Property—TFP (see also TFP Student Action), 4, 14n., 28-30,

191, 202, 213

Transgender, 8n, 26, 29, 61n.

Tremblay, Pierre, 114-115

Tripp, C. C., 87

TV commercials, use in movement's tactics, 37

Twins, identical, *and homosexuality*, 84-85

Ugandan Martyrs, 185-186

Unperceived Ideological Transshipment, 17n

US National Religious GLBT Organizations, 26n

Usher, Rod, 13n.

Varnell, Paul, 8-9, 19, 54

Vice(s), *correlation of all*, 160; *State's obligation to proscribe*, 97, 196-197; *turned into gods*, 59

Victims of homosexual lifestyle, 115

Victims, homosexuals portrayed as, 36-37

Violence, domestic, *among homosexuals*, 106, 110-111, 115

Virgin Mary, portrayed as a lesbian, 188

Virtue(s), *correlation of all*, 129, 160; *homosexuality presented as*, 49-50; *State enforcement of the practice of*, 97, 196

Voeller, Bruce, 40

Weinberg, George, 35

Weinberg, Martin S., 109n

Whitehead, Neil and Briar, 87

Xiridou, Maria, 107

Young, Allen, 81n

The American Society for the Defense of Tradition, Family and Property (TFP) was born of a group of Catholic Americans concerned about the multiple crises shaking every aspect of American life. Founded in 1973, the American TFP was formed to resist, in the realm of ideas, the liberal, socialist and communist trends of the times and proudly affirm the positive values of tradition, family and property. Central to the TFP mission is the idea that the various crises threatening American society and the Catholic Church cannot be seen as separate and disjointed events but rather must be seen as the consequences of a worldwide crisis based on the errors of our times. The TFP handbook *Revolution and Counter-Revolution* by Plinio Corrêa de Oliveira masterfully traces the historical and philosophical roots of the present crisis and proposes a response.

Thus, the TFP is a movement that embraces every field of action, especially in art, ideas and culture. TFP books, publications and newspaper advertisements help bring these views to the public. Moreover, the TFP takes issues to the streets with colorful sidewalk campaigns in major cities.

The first TFP was founded in Brazil in 1960 by Prof. Plinio Corrêa de Oliveira. The American TFP is one of many autonomous TFPs that now exist around the world dedicated to the same ideals and at the service of Christian Civilization. The American TFP's national headquarters is located in Spring Grove, Pennsylvania.

The TFP Committee on American Issues is a study commission recently set up to monitor events in American society and the Church. It issues papers and articles that frequently appear on the TFP website. For more information on the TFP please visit its website at **www.tfp.org**.

Nobility and Analogous Traditional Elites in the Allocutions of Pius XII:
A Theme Illuminating American Social History
   by *Plinio Corrêa de Oliveira*

Since the eighteenth century, generations have been schooled in utopian principles proclaiming total equality as the guarantor of liberty and justice for all. The egalitarian myth of a classless society was proffered as the unquestionable path down which mankind must travel to reach perfect social harmony. This book does much to shatter these myths and provide a Catholic approach to the way society should be structured as seen by the Popes.

592 pages, hardcover, 64 full-color pictures, 52 black-and-white pictures, Hamilton Press, ©1993. **$49.95**

Revolution and Counter-Revolution
   by *Plinio Corrêa de Oliveira*

If anything characterizes our times, it is a sense of pervading chaos. In every field of human endeavor, the windstorms of change are fast altering the ways we live. Contemporary man is no longer anchored in certainties and thus has lost sight of who he is, where he comes from and where he is going. If there is a single book that can shed light amid the postmodern darkness, this is it.

180 pages, paperback, American Society for the Defense of Tradition, Family, and Property (TFP), ©2003. **$9.95**

To order please call: **1-***(866) 661-0272*

The Crusader of the 20th Century
by *Roberto de Mattei*

"With the integrity of his life as an authentic Catholic, Plinio Corrêa de Oliveira offers us a confirmation of the Church's continuing fecundity. The difficulties of these times for true Catholics are, in fact, occasions to influence history by affirming perennial Christian principles. Such was the case with Professor Plinio, the eminent Brazilian thinker who demonstrated it by boldly maintaining, in an age of totalitarianism of every stripe and color, his unshakable faith in the fundamental teachings and institutions of the Church." From the Introduction by Alfonso Cardinal Stickler.

First Edition, 278 pages, hardcover, ©1998. **$14.95**

I Have Weathered Other Storms:
A Response to the Scandals and Democratic Reforms that Threaten the Catholic Church
by *TFP Committee on American Issues*

Cut through the media hype and intense emotion! I Have Weathered Other Storms is a response to the current sexual-abuse scandals that goes right to the core of the problem.

Powerfully documented, fully indexed and richly illustrated, this 180-page book delves into the profound crisis of Faith, media blitz and bias, and a reformists' agenda for changing the Church.

Must reading for all Catholics concerned with the present crisis. An arsenal of Church doctrine and teachings you can use.

This book put the crisis in a much-needed supernatural perspective. The Church is not just any organization; it has indeed weathered other storms.

First Edition, 192 pages, paperback, ©2002. **$12.95**

To order please call: 1-*(866) 661-0272*